Taylor's Guides to Gardening

Roger Holmes, Editor

Frances Tenenbaum, Series Editor

HOUGHTON MIFFLIN COMPANY
Boston • New York   1997

Taylor's Guide to Ornamental Grasses

For information about permission to reproduce selections from this book, write to Permissions, Houghton Mifflin Company, 215 Park Avenue South, New York, New York 10003.

For information about this and other Houghton Mifflin trade and reference books and multimedia products, visit The Bookstore at Houghton Mifflin on the World Wide Web at http://www.hmco.com/trade/.

Taylor's Guide is a registered trademark of Houghton Mifflin Company.

Library of Congress Cataloging-in-Publication Data
Taylor's guide to ornamental grasses / Roger Holmes, editor.
    p. cm. — (Taylor's guides to gardening)
   Includes index.
   ISBN 0-395-79761-6
   1. Ornamental grasses. I. Holmes, Roger. II. Series.
SB431.7.T39 1997
   635.9'64—dc20   96-38427

Printed in Hong Kong

DNP 10 9 8 7 6 5 4

Cover photograph © by Jerry Pavia

Contents

Contributors

Sally Roth selected the plants to include in this book and wrote the essays and plant descriptions in the encyclopedia. She contributed to *Taylor's Guide to Fruits and Berries* and has written extensively on gardening in books and magazine articles. She is a contributing editor to *Fine Gardening* magazine and writes a weekly nature column for the *Evansville Courier*. She has studied native grasses and grown ornamental grasses in Pennsylvania, Oregon, and at her current home in New Harmony, Indiana.

Roger Holmes edited this book, ably assisted by Sarah Disbrow. He was coeditor (with Rita Buchanan) of *Taylor's Master Guide to Gardening* and several other titles in the Taylor's Guide series. He lives in Lincoln, Nebraska.

Consultants

Pierre Bennerup provided advice on *Acorus, Carex, Juncus,* and *Koeleria,* among other genera in this book. He is the owner of Sunny Border Nurseries, Inc., in Kensington, Connecticut, wholesale suppliers of grasses and other plants. He is also the owner of Comstock, Ferre & Co., in Wethersfield, Connecticut, the oldest seed company in the United States.

Kurt Bluemel offered suggestions on the genera *Festuca* and *Miscanthus.* He is owner of Kurt Bluemel, Inc., in Baldwin, Maryland, a mail-order nursery specializing in ornamental grasses and companion perennials. Through his lectures and appearances, he has been a major influence in the increasing use of ornamental grasses in American gardens. He has also introduced several fine new cultivars.

Carmen R. Hardin reviewed information about native prairie grasses, including *Andropogon, Schizachyrium, Sporobolus,* and others. She is general manager of CRM Ecosystems, Inc., in Mt. Horeb, Wisconsin, a native seed and plant nursery for the Great Lakes region specializing in consultation, restoration, and management of native ecosystems including prairies, woodlands, and wetlands.

Norm Hooven offered comments on *Calamagrostis, Melica, Milium, Molinia,* and other genera. He and his wife, Phyllis, are owners of Limerock Ornamental Grasses, Inc., in Port Matilda, Pennsylvania, a mail-order nursery specializing in ornamental and native grasses, rushes, sedges, and companion perennials.

Wayne Pauly supplied information on using fire as a maintenance tool for prairie plantings. He is a naturalist for the Dane County Park Commission in Madison, Wisconsin, and author of *How to Manage Small Prairie Fires,* available for a small fee from the Dane County Park Commission, 4318 Robertson Road, Madison, WI 53714.

Mark Stromberg offered advice about the native western grasses in this book, including *Bouteloua, Deschampsia, Stipa,* and other genera, and he provided up-to-date cautions on exotic grasses that are or may be invasive in the West. His extensive association with grasses includes work for the Nature Conservancy in Wyoming, Colorado, and New Mexico, and for the National Audubon Society grassland sanctuary in southeastern Arizona. He is currently manager of the University of California at Berkeley's Hastings Reserve, an oak savanna in central coastal California, and is president of the California Native Grass Association.

Mark Trela consulted on *Equisetum, Erianthus, Thypha, Zea,* and other genera. He is vice president of Fragrant Farms in New Harmony, Indiana, overseeing 25 acres of organically grown flowers, grasses, and other plants for the cut-flower market and dried arrangements.

How to Use This Guide

Grasses are among the most versatile garden and landscape plants, at home with annuals, perennials, and shrubs in mixed beds and borders; planted as individual specimens; massed over large areas; or whispering in the breeze above a patio planter. Ornamental grasses are also relatively new to many gardeners, who will find here a useful introduction. More experienced readers will find here a handy and up-to-date source of information on dozens and dozens of grasses, many of which were unavailable a decade ago.

How This Guide Is Organized

Like many of the books in this series, this one contains essays and a large selection of plants shown on color plates and described in an encyclopedia.

The essays

Three essays present an overview of ornamental grasses. In the first, we introduce the grasses and their close relatives, sedges and rushes, and examine their characteristics and appeal. The second essay looks at how these qualities contribute to garden and landscape situations. Photos on pages 46–113 illustrate the concepts discussed in this essay.

The plants

Recent years have seen a tremendous increase in the range of ornamental grasses available to homeowners. In this book we present a large number (nearly 200) of these. Almost all offer handsome foliage, striking form, and attractive texture. Many produce eye-catching flowers (small individually but impressive in the aggregate) and/or seed heads, and most provide interest in at least two seasons. Local nurseries are responding to increased interest in ornamental grasses, but still stock only a few varieties; all the plants in the book are likely to be available from one or more of the mail-order suppliers listed in "Sources of Supply" at the end of the book.

Gallery of grasses

To help you choose individual plants, the photos in this section will give you a good idea of a plant's foliage, form, and other attractive qualities. A short comment on the plant's use or character accompanies each plate, along with the page on which you'll find its encyclopedia entry.

Encyclopedia of grasses

If you're intrigued by a plant mentioned in an essay, shown in the Gallery, or that you see in a friend's garden, consult this section. The encyclopedia contains descriptions of each plant shown in the color plates as well as a great many additional cultivars and related species. The listings are arranged alphabetically by genus. (If you don't know the botanical name, look up the species by common name in the index.)

Each genus is briefly described, followed by detailed descriptions of selected species and cultivars. These entries present the plant's desirable qualities (and sometimes problematic ones), provide suggestions for using it, and comment on how to grow it.

A Note on Hardiness Zones

Plants vary considerably in their ability to withstand cold temperatures. Those native to high-elevation northern regions, for instance, can survive bitter cold, many degrees below zero, while some tropical plants may die when touched by the slightest frost. In the early years of this century horticulturists began to correlate the cold hardiness of plants with gradients of temperature as plotted on a map. The zone map on pp. 288–289 is based on one recently revised by the USDA, which represents 10 temperature zones for North America. The zone ratings given for each plant indicate the lowest temperatures the plant can usually be expected to survive. A plant rated Zone 5, for instance, should survive minimum temperatures between -10 to -20°F.

When selecting plants, remember that hardiness zone ratings don't account for other important factors, such as heat and wind. These factors are mentioned in the plant descriptions; if you're in doubt about a plant's suitability for your location, ask a knowledgeable person at your local nursery.

Gardening with Grasses

Not so long ago, a patch of ribbon grass by the back door or a clump of Eulalia grass standing sentry in the front yard was about as decorative as grasses got on residential properties. For most homeowners, and many gardeners, grass was the stuff they mowed every week, and the only grass in the garden was the lawn clippings spread among annuals and perennials as mulch.

Today, grasses appear in every corner of the home landscape. From neat tuffets of sheep's fescue, as springy to the touch as a pad of steel wool, to towering plumes of giant Chinese silver grass rising above a dense column of lush leaves, there is a grass that will suit any need. In beds and borders, some jostle for attention as specimen plants while others provide a backdrop for showier neighbors. Grasses dapple a meadow planting with splashes of gold, sway invitingly on the edge of a pond, and secure the soil on a steep bank. In a pot, a spray of arching leaves graces a patio. Planted en masse, grasses are the equal of many shrub borders and can be as effective, and much quicker, in creating privacy as the densest hedge. In all these situations, grasses can offer something special — changing colors and forms, flowers, seed heads — in each season. And if that isn't recommendation enough, grasses are among the easiest plants to grow, adapting easily to a wide range of conditions in the home landscape, where they are untroubled by pests and diseases.

What Is an Ornamental Grass?

Almost any grass can be decorative in the right place, but the ones commonly considered ornamental have a special appeal of texture, form, and color.

Foliage is the key to that appeal. Grass leaves or blades come in wonderful variations, from flat or pleated, bent or rolled to straight-edged, wavy, or wiry. These pleasing shapes often play a role in the plant's survival. Rolled or folded leaves, for example, preserve moisture in dry climates, while broad leaves capture scarce sunlight in shady locations. The varied foliage produces equally impressive plant shapes, from neat and springy fuzzcuts to gracefully flowing manes. Tufted grasses are usually the shortest, with thin, dense, spiky leaves. Mounded grasses have a smooth, flowing outline, like a water-worn boulder, an effect produced by leaves bowing over to the ground. Taller than mounds, arching grasses curve gracefully downward like the spray of a fountain. Upright grasses have a strong vertical line, with the leaves either in a tight column or a more relaxed V shape.

Many grasses exhibit two shapes at once, or they may change shape as the leaves elongate or the plant begins to flower. Some arching grasses bend only a few inches at the top, the rest of the plant remaining staunchly upright. Mounded grasses may gain an upright aspect when punctuated by tall flower stems. And many taller grasses, like the gardeners who tend them, stand upright early in the season and bend over as they age.

For many gardeners, the glory of ornamental grasses is color. From brilliant reds and golds to quieter earth tones and infinite shades of green, grass foliage can dazzle or soothe the eye. Likewise, variegated leaves (striped or edged in color) can shimmer softly or pulse brilliantly. Unlike perennials, which usually fade into oblivion at the end of the season, grasses are often at their peak of color during dormancy, when foliage mellows to tawny golds and warm beiges. As dormancy deepens, leaves gradually bleach to shades of tan and platinum.

While grasses are prized for their foliage, many also flower dramatically. Individual flowers are tiny, but clustered together they can be spectacular. Some have long, silken flower clusters that often ripen to puffs; others have spiky clusters, or plumes that look like giant feather dusters. Depending on type, grasses may flower in spring or fall. (See the discussion of warm- and cool-season grasses later in this chapter.) The flowers often last for weeks before giving way to seed heads, which are distinctive in their own right. Long after birds or wind have dispersed the seeds, seed heads persist, usually pretty enough to leave standing through the winter.

Grasses for Garden and Landscape

Of the thousands of grasses and grasslike plants with distinct ornamental appeal, we have selected several hundred for this book based on their beauty and usefulness in the garden or landscape. Included are true grasses and bamboos, grasslike sedges and rushes, and a few other plants resembling grass in looks and landscape use. We've drawn the line at grasslike plants such as alliums and daylilies that are valued primarily for their bloom. Ornamental grasses are increasingly available at local nurseries, but the selection is still likely to be limited. Because of this, we've done our best to ensure that all the plants in this book can be purchased from mail-order suppliers. (Consult the listing in this book, or ask your nursery to order for you.)

True grasses and bamboos

The family of true grasses, Graminae (also called Poaceae), is a conglomerate of 700 genera and 7,000 species that includes pasture and meadow grasses, cereal grasses, forage and fodder grasses, even grass used as timber (bamboo), as well as horticultural grasses grown as ornamentals.

All true grasses are monocots, producing a single seed leaf and mature leaves with parallel veins. (Most other plants are dicots, which have two seed leaves.) The stems or culms of a grass plant are hollow, except in a few species, with solid joints, or nodes. Bamboos, which range from miniature potted specimens to 40-foot timber giants, have prominent stems. But stems of other grasses aren't always apparent. Many are visible only at flowering time, when the culms lengthen and emerge from the tuft of grass.

In addition to their beauty, leaves of true grasses have an unusual characteristic familiar to anyone who has to mow the lawn every week — they continue to grow after being cut. Most plants have their growth points near the tips of the leaves and branches. Grasses grow from special cells located near their attachment to the stem, a survival adaptation to millennia of grazing and fires. Grass leaves are so eye-catching that they invite touching as well. While some are a delight to stroke, with velvety leaves as soft as a baby's downy cheek, others hide an arsenal of defenses. A look under a strong hand lens at prairie cord grass, for example, will reveal fine, serrated edges that can rip your skin if you stroke the leaf in the wrong direction.

The minuscule flowers of grasses cluster together, arranged on a stem in a tight spike, held separately on the thin stems of a raceme, or fanned out on the branching stems of a panicle, as shown on the facing page. Lacking petals to attract bees and other pollinators, grass flowers are fertilized by grains of pollen carried on the wind. Shake a head of timothy grass in bloom and you'll set free a smokelike puff of pollen, a floating sneeze waiting to happen. Flowers are held within spikelets of overlapping bracts. A hairlike awn may extend from the tip of each bract, giving the seed head a bristly or hairy look (think of a head of wheat). Sometimes the awns are extremely long and catch the light like strands of silk. When the seed head shatters, the awns wind into tight coils, propelling the sharp-pointed seed into the soil. Some grasses are both prized and reviled for their long awns, which make the grass shimmer like silver but have the nasty habit of lodging in sweaters and socks, and in the ears, nose, throat, and feet of family dogs and cats.

Sedges and rushes

In the wild, rushes and sedges are among the first to colonize wet spots. In the garden, they are ideal for filling difficult spots in wet soil or in shade. These grasslike monocots from the family Cyperacea can be difficult to distinguish from true grasses at first glance, but a closer examination will reveal differences. Most plants in this family have three-angled stems, which accounts for the old catch phrase "sedges have edges." Though a few species of rushes and sedges have round stems like grasses, the inside of the stem is pithy rather than hollow.

Most sedges grow in arching or erect clumps, while most rushes are travelers, spreading by creeping roots. As with true grasses, habit and form vary by species. While nearly all sedges and rushes prefer wet or boggy soil, some also adapt to average garden conditions.

Making Choices

Until recently, gardeners had limited choices among grasses. Plants now popular and widely available, like Japanese blood grass, were virtually unknown only 10 years ago. Today the challenge isn't finding grasses to grow, it's choosing from among the many available. Before you introduce it into your garden, you'll want to know whether a grass is an annual or a perennial, whether it grows in a tight clump or spreads

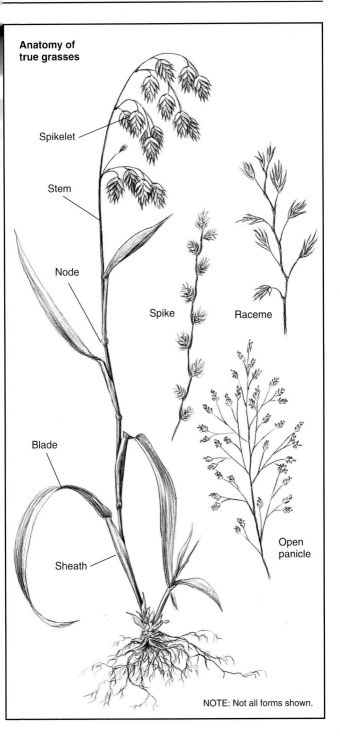

**Anatomy of
true grasses**

Spikelet

Stem

Node

Spike

Raceme

Blade

Open
panicle

Sheath

NOTE: Not all forms shown.

rapidly by runners, and whether it grows in the cool or warm seasons.

Annuals and perennials

Annual grasses sprout, flower, set seed, and die in a single year, while perennials are in for the long haul (some living for a hundred years or more). Though there are some biennial grasses too, they are not commonly available, even from specialty nurseries, and are therefore not included in this book.

You can sow annual grasses in a garden as you would flowering annuals. Their flowers and seed heads are showy in the summer garden and stunning in an autumn vase. Annuals are also appealing in a meadow garden or a naturalized planting, where they are free spirits, self-sowing among other plants.

Where you want a permanent landscape feature, such as a screen or hedge, or in a mixed border, perennial grasses are the better choice. Many grasses require you to take the word "permanent" to heart, growing enormous root systems that are all but impossible to pry out once they've settled in. You can still see century-old clumps of pampas grass so well rooted that homeowners who've inherited them have little option but to build gardens around them. The popular miscanthus grasses, of which there are dozens of cultivated varieties, are particularly long lived.

Some perennial grasses are less permanent. Pennisetums and blue fescues are sensitive to rot over the winter and can die out suddenly after thriving for several years. Others, including the lovely crimson fountain grass (*Pennisetum setaceum* 'Rubrum'), are not cold-hardy or heat-tolerant. These grasses might best be grown as annuals, just as we grow tender perennials like impatiens as annual flowers.

Root systems

You needn't consider roots of annual grasses, which die along with the plant after a single season. Roots of some perennial grasses, as indicated above, can be tenacious, and you should think before introducing these grasses to gardens. Chin-high prairie types, for example, can dig down twice as deep as their height. Such grasses may pose problems for neighboring plants by outcompeting them for scarce water. If you like to rearrange your borders or landscape, these grasses can also be a chore to move.

Even more important than the size of roots are the ways in which they travel. Running grasses spread above ground by stolons or below ground by rhizomes, rooting along the way. Bunching or clumping grasses expand their territory by shoots that keep the plant in a compact clump.

Be extremely wary of introducing running grasses into a garden bed. If you've ever weeded quack grass from among your favorite flowers, you know how difficult it is to remove the stubborn roots of running grasses. And don't be fooled by slow growth the first year. An old saying says, "The first year it sleeps, the second year it creeps, the third year it leaps." Because they root together to form a dense sod, running grasses are better used for lawns or extended ground covers. If you must have them in a border, confine them within deep vertical barriers or plant them in pots. Climate can affect the spread of invasive species. Running grasses are thirsty plants and their travels are curtailed where water is scarce.

Clumping grasses, on the other hand, make ideal ornamentals in garden beds or specimens in the landscape. The clumps expand slowly over the years, never taking over the border. Planted close together, clumping grasses may look like a solid stretch of running grass, but a close examination of the roots will reassure you that each plant is well defined and separated from its neighbor.

Warm- and cool-season grasses

Ranchers noticed long before gardeners that some grasses grow best in spring and fall, while others thrive in summer heat. These different schedules of photosynthesis evolved as a response to climate. Where summers are hot and bone-dry and winters mild, the native grasses go dormant, waiting for autumn rains before they green up again. Grasses like this are called cool-season grasses because they thrive in cool, moist weather, when the temperature hits about 65°F. They come alive in winter or early spring and flower from late winter to early summer, depending on species. After the seed ripens, they go dormant for the summer, sleeping until the seasons change again. Warm-season grasses, on the other hand, sprout up in spring, after the air and soil are warm. They flourish through the heat of summer, growing best when the thermometer climbs above 80°F. They flower in summer and fall. In fall or winter, they begin dormancy.

Most ornamental grasses are warm-season types. They grow lush throughout the summer, when the garden is at its peak, and offer a burst of late-season color and interest when they push up flowers. Warm-season grasses take on beautiful color for fall and winter, in shades of gold, tan, red, and even orange. As the plants sink deeper into dormancy, the foliage bleaches in the weather to hues of tan or straw and stiffens into its winter silhouette. Cool-season grasses are good for meadows or naturalistic plantings, and they offer early appeal in a border. In mild climates, their foliage is evergreen, at least over the winter season, and the leaves often take on hints of red and purple or yellow in cool weather. Some cool-season grasses bloom in spring but stay decorative in the garden for months. Feather reed grass *(Calamagrostis acutiflora* var. *stricta),* for example, flowers in spring, but the golden spikes persist well into summer.

Transplanted from their natural, mild-winter climate to colder regions, cool-season grasses can behave like warm-season grasses, going dormant in the winter and waiting until spring to venture new growth. Summer dormancy can sometimes be staved off with regular watering, or by cutting back spent seed heads. Warm-season grasses can also produce surprises outside their natural setting. When the warm-season zoysia grass, which looks great in Florida and the Southeast, was transplanted to northern lawns, homeowners soon found that their green carpet turned brown at the first touch of cold weather — and stayed that way until late spring. Many of those zoysia plugs were pulled up and replanted with a more suitable grass.

Considerations of dormancy, foliage color, and flowering times aside, the warm or cool nature of a grass shouldn't affect its ability to survive in your garden. Warm- or cool-season grasses can be grown wherever they are cold-hardy, unless humidity or other extremes of climate are not to their liking (see encyclopedia listings for such cases). But keep in mind their seasonal nature. If your area is prone to long dry spells in summer, cool-season grasses will go naturally dormant, but actively growing warm-season grasses may need supplemental watering. If your winters are long and cold, your cool-season grasses may wait until the weather breaks before they begin to green up.

Sampling Grasses

Grasses have become so popular so quickly that a drive through town may be the simplest way to discover grasses that you'd like to have in your own garden. City dwellers can often find imaginative grass plantings along roadsides, in parks, at botanical gardens, or on the grounds of institutions or businesses. Repeat the trip every month or so to observe the transformations each season brings to the grasses you see. Washington, D.C., has many public gardens built around grasses, among them the work of landscape architects Wolfgang Oehme and James van Sweden, whose designs have been instrumental in the recent surge of interest in grasses. Some institutions, such as the Santa Barbara Botanic Garden and the Strybing Arboretum, both in California, include "wild" landscapes planted with native grasses and wildflowers. A visit to a prairie restoration in the Midwest offers the chance to experience something of the awe of early settlers who gazed upon an endless sea of grass.

Another way to immerse yourself in grass selections is a trip to a nursery that specializes in grasses, if you have the good fortune to live near one. (The resources section on page 290 includes addresses.) For those who don't, mail-order catalogs have the best grass offerings, but their simple lists, sparse descriptions, and limited photos can be a letdown if you're used to perennial catalogs. The best approach is to flag the grasses you like in this book, then search for the plants by botanical name in a catalog. Grasses are often known by more than one botanical name, so we've included alternate names in the encyclopedia entries to help in your catalog search.

Local nurseries won't have the breadth of selection of a good mail-order specialist, but more are including grasses in their demonstration plantings. Many local nurseries will be happy to special-order plants from wholesale distributors, and creating demand will bring more plants to local outlets where you can see the real thing before buying. If you order from your local nursery, be sure to supply them with the botanical name of the plant and any cultivar name, so you get what you expect.

Grasses in the Landscape

Striking foliage, clouds of blossom, glimmering highlights, music and motion — ornamental grasses are among the most rewarding and challenging landscape plants. Tall upright grasses make terrific specimen or accent plants in formal gardens. Arches or spills do the same for the casual garden. Low mounds and tight clumps are self-contained enough for rock gardens or edgings, and running grasses spread out for a soft effect as a ground cover.

Grasses also combine well with flowers, shrubs, and vines in borders, and they make excellent fast-growing screens, graceful buffers along the hard surfaces of walls and walks, and pretty potted plants. There are grasses for wet or boggy sites like water gardens and ponds, as well as for water-saving xeriscapes.

The wisest way to plan a landscape with grasses is to combine what you see and like in a grass with the knowledge of its general behavior and the requirements of your design. In this chapter we will discuss ways to use specific grasses in the landscape and offer suggestions for striking combinations with other plants.

Designing with Grasses

Before we look at specific landscaping situations, a few general comments about designing with grasses may be helpful. Grasses have distinctive silhouettes, often of striking size, that run the gamut in attitude from loose, floppy, and informal, to erect or compact and formal. Use these attitudes to impart or reinforce the character you desire for a planting. Be aware that site and companions can alter the feel of a plant. Set beside a doorstep or anchoring the end of a border, the tall, bare, flowering stems of the tall moor grass 'Skyracer' *(Molinia caerulea* ssp. *litoralis)* stand like a formal sentry. But dotted about a wild meadow design or set among perennials and succulents on a rocky hillside, clumps of 'Skyracer' blend right in.

Grasses grow fast, some approaching full size in a single season, and you can't prune or pinch them to keep them in bounds. So consider the mature size of the plant when placing it. Consider also its shape when in flower. In spring or fall (depending on the grass), flowering stems may suddenly rise well above the foliage, blocking the view of plants behind.

Designing with grasses, like all ornamental plants, requires consideration of foliage, color, and texture, and we'll discuss those qualities below. Most other plants, however, lack two of the most pleasing characteristics of grass: sound and motion. Grasses bow and dance in the breeze, each singing a characteristic song. Tall, wide-bladed grasses sigh deeply in a wind, while those with finer leaves sing a softer, higher note. As foliage dries and stiffens in dormancy, it emits a harsher, sharper rattle. Take advantage of this song and dance just as you do the fragrance and color of other plants.

Finally, when you design with grasses keep in mind that they don't fade into oblivion at the end of the growing season. Many gardeners think of fall as the best season for grasses. The warm golden tones set off colorful fall flowers and foliage beautifully. In colder climates, when fall turns to winter, grasses continue to add color and motion. Dormant grasses contrast handsomely with evergreen and berry-laden shrubs, while evergreen grasses, such as some bamboos and rushes, stand out in a sleeping landscape. Set against the pale leaves and soft plumes of a grass, the blackened seed pods of spent perennials form a lovely picture of contrasting line and color.

Grasses as Specimen and Accent Plants

Some grasses are so assertive in stature, shape, and color that they naturally create a focal point. Of all these qualities, height is the most impressive. Tall grasses make some of the best specimens simply because they're impossible to overlook. Giant cane *(Arundo donax),* which reaches up to 25 feet, and cultivars of miscanthus and pampas grasses that reach 12 to 15 feet draw attention anywhere, especially when they're in bloom. A sense of proportion is needed when using these giants — they're too often seen towering precariously over much smaller perennials like Gulliver among the Lilliputians.

Some tall specimens have enough presence to stand alone, while others do better in a group. A single *Miscanthus sinensis* 'Cosmopolitan', with its broad, striped leaves, can anchor an entryway all by itself. But it may take three or five pampas grass plants *(Cortaderia selloana),* even with their towering feather-duster flowers, to set off a low ranch house. If you want to use a lanky grass such as giant cane as an accent, plant it as a screen or hedge at least 15 feet long to allow the plants to look architectural rather than awkward. To make a

---

Fine specimen grasses

Arundo donax (Giant reed)

Calamagrostis acutiflora 'Stricta' ('Stricta' feather reed grass)

Chasmanthium latifolium (Northern sea oats)

Erianthus ravennae (Ravenna grass)

Hakonechloa macra 'Aureola' (Golden hakonechloa)

Miscanthus floridulus (Giant Chinese silver grass)

Miscanthus sacchariflorus (Silver banner grass)

Miscanthus sinensis, all cultivars

   M. sinensis 'Strictus' (Porcupine grass)

   M. sinensis 'Variegatus' (Striped Eulalia grass)

   M. sinensis 'Zebrinus' (Zebra grass)

Molinia caerulea (Purple moor grass)

Panicum virgatum, species and cultivars (Switch grass)

Pennisetum macrostachyum 'Burgundy Giant'

Pennisetum alopecuroides (Australian fountain grass)

Pennisetum orientale (Oriental fountain grass)

Pennisetum setaceum (Crimson fountain grass)

Spodiopogon sibiricus

Interesting grasses for containers

Cymbopogon citratus (Lemon grass)
Cyperus spp. and cvs. (Papyrus)
Juncus spp. (Rushes)
Koeleria glauca (Large blue hair grass)
Helictotrichon sempervirens (Blue oat grass)
Pennisetum setaceum 'Rubrum' (Crimson fountain grass)

single specimen or a group stand out even more, plant it against a dark background or at the water's edge for high-lighting. The fine blades of 'Morning Light' miscanthus form a green fountain that contrasts with darker firs or spruces. When autumn comes and the grass mellows to the color of ripe wheat, the planting will light up like a sunburst.

Planted en masse, shorter grasses can make excellent focal points. All cultivars of switch grass *(Panicum virgatum)* are attention-getters in a mass planting, especially when they raise their airy, light-catching flowers. *Spodiopogon sibiricus,* with its leaves held at right angles to the stem, is another good candidate for mass planting. Shorter grasses make fine accents on a patio or along walks, walls, and fences. Pot them in containers or plant them in the ground along the edges. Line a walk with the delicate panicles of hairy melic grass *(Melica ciliata)* or plant ribbon grass *(Phalaris arundinacea* 'Picta') against a stone wall or around a flagstone patio. If it gets ragged, simply mow it down, water deeply, and let it regrow.

Grasses in Flower Beds and Borders

Gardening books are filled with time-tested combinations of annuals and perennials for the flower border, but designing a mixed border with grasses is relatively new. That leaves plenty of room to experiment. As newcomers to the border, grasses not only freshen a staid arrangement — a shimmer of fountain grass above lamb's-ears will show off the plant in a new way — they also improve a border's appearance in the off-season. The leftover seedpods and woody stems of perennials such as black-eyed Susan and purple coneflower are much more dramatic against the bleached leaves and soft seed plumes of grasses.

If you're adding ornamental grasses to an established bed or border, keep in mind that grasses are by nature thrifty plants, flourishing in soils that are lean in fertility and poor in texture. When they move into the loose, rich, deep soil of a prepared perennial bed or border, it's like switching from a futon to a featherbed. Too much of a good thing can make them weak and floppy. A leaner diet creates a stockier, shorter, more compact plant, which is usually what gardeners prefer. The grasses that do best in a rich bed are low or medium-high clumping grasses with a natural fountainlike habit. They'll maintain an attractive shape even if they get an energy boost from improved garden soil. Running grasses will take off through a collection of cherished perennials faster than you can say stop, and upright cultivars of tall grasses are likely to put on unusual height or fall apart. If you want to plant these tall grasses in your border, stake the tall ones up or plant them behind the prepared soil of the border proper.

In many ways, grasses are just like perennials when it comes to combinations for the border. There are choices that contrast dramatically with neighboring plants, those that complement other plants by showing off their color or shape to best effect, and some that echo their form, texture, or color. The following discussions cover some of the ways you can combine grasses and other perennials in the border.

Studied contrasts

The fine blades of most grasses look good against plants with large leaves, immense stature, or oversize flowers. If your taste tends to the extremes, try combining a tall grass of fine to medium texture, such as 'Sarabande' or 'Gracillimus' miscanthus, with the scallop-leaved plume poppy *(Macleaya cordata)*. The extravagantly large foliage of *Rodgersia* or *Rheum,* often difficult to work into the garden, can be gracefully melded with other perennials if it's brought down to size with neighboring grasses. Tall red swamp hibiscus *(Hibiscus coccineus)* is an inspired combination with a mound of *Miscanthus floridulus,* a substantial grass with strappy foliage. In summer, the lobed leaves and brilliant red hibiscus flowers shine against the green of the grass. In autumn, cupped seedpods stand out against bleached foliage and fluffy plumes. On a less extreme scale, hostas, bergenias, and other plants with good-sized, simple leaves also make fine companions for ornamental grasses.

Combining for color

Most grasses have colors that harmonize well. Their cool green or blue tones brighten the pinks, purples, or yellows of perennials, giving these colors more mileage in the garden. A few cheddar pinks *(Dianthus gratianopoltanus),* for instance, interspersed in a spreading mat of springy blue fescue *(Festuca cinerea* 'Elijah's Blue' or other cultivars), have more impact than a solid planting of pinks.

Variegated grasses, with their cool whitened leaves, are beautiful with all kinds of border flowers. Variegated miscanthus (*Miscanthus sinensis* 'Variegatus') is perfect for the mixed perennial border, where its whitish green foliage provides a good foil for garden phlox and other perennials. And by the time the miscanthus flowers in early autumn, its rose pink panicles are a solo star in the border. The hot pink, salmon, and red flowers of coralbells (*Heuchera* spp.) show up vividly against ghostly white-green grasses, such as variegated bulbous oat grass (*Arrhenatherum elatius* var. *bulbosum* 'Variegatum'). Heucheras with deep-colored or fancy-leaved foliage, such as 'Palace Purple' and 'Pewter Veil', are standouts with plain green or gold-green grasses. Brilliant cerise phlox or any strong pink cultivar is made even more shocking when set against old-fashioned ribbon grass, and these garden phloxes can hold their own against the running grass.

Ornamental grasses can tame as well as brighten the colors around them. If you find your pink poppies have too much orange in them to look good next to the cool pink phlox, provide a visual interlude of restful green or gray-green grasses between them. The spiky leaves of small Japanese silver grass *(Miscanthus oligostachys),* which stick out from the neat clump at almost right angles, make a good intermediary in the mixed border, adding lively texture but quiet color. A blue-gray-leaved cultivar of little bluestem (*Schizachyrium scoparium* 'The Blues') is another outstanding mid-height grass to settle into a mixed border.

Not all grasses mix easily. Those in the red range, with maroon or wine red leaves or hints of bright red, are a little trickier to combine with perennials. If the red tends to brown, try white or blue flowers with it; if it has a more purple undertone, go for pinks and purples as well. Grasses with yellow stripes, such as 'Goldfeder' miscanthus (*Miscanthus sinensis* 'Goldfeder'), have a warm tone that goes well with yellows and blues but clashes with most pinks. The cooler grasses with white-striped or white-edged leaves, like variegated bulbous oat grass (*Arrhenatherum elatius* var. *bulbosum* 'Variegatum') or variegated pampas grass (*Cortaderia selloana* 'Silver Comet'), make a good foil for pink, red, and white flowers, but are not so pleasing with yellow tones.

If you want to coordinate bloom times of grasses and perennials, remember that cool-season grasses bloom in the spring or early summer when the rest of the garden is also hitting its peak. By July, the show is over. Warm-season grasses burst into bloom in the fall. To be sure blooms will coincide, choose late-blooming flowers like asters or mums to accompany them. Remember to consider the height of flowering stems in relation to other plants in the border. Some grasses

Well-behaved grasses for the border

Achnatherum calamagrostis (Silver spike grass)
Agropyron magellanicum (Blue Magellan grass)
Briza media (Perennial quaking grass)
Carex buchananii (Leather-leaf sedge)
Carex comans (New Zealand hair sedge)
Carex plantaginea (Plantain-leaved sedge)
Festuca spp. and cvs. (Fescues)
Hakonechloa spp. and cvs. (Hakonechloa grass)
Helictotrichon sempervirens and cvs. (Blue oat grass)
Miscanthus floridulus (Giant Chinese silver grass)
Miscanthus sinensis, any cultivar, particularly:
   M. sinensis 'Strictus' (Porcupine grass)
   M. sinensis 'Variegatus' (Striped Eulalia grass)
   M. sinensis 'Zebrinus' (Zebra grass)
Molinia spp. and cvs. (Moor grass)
Muhlenbergia pubescens (Soft blue Mexican muhly)
Pennisetum alopecuroides 'Hameln'
   ('Hameln' fountain grass)
Pennisetum orientale (Oriental fountain grass)
Phalaris arundinacea 'Dwarf Garters'
   (Dwarf ribbon grass)
Phormium tenax (New Zealand flax)
Spodiopogon sibiricus (Frost grass)

Grasses to avoid in a border

These grasses spread aggressively by roots or stolons.
They can become a serious problem in the border:

Acorus gramineus and its cultivars (Japanese sweet flag)
Ammophila arenaria (European beach grass)
Arundinaria viridistrata (Running bamboo)
Buchloe dactyloides (Buffalo grass)
Elymus arenarius and cultivars (Blue Lyme grass)
Equisetum hyemale (Scouring rush)
Glyceria maxima and *G. m.* 'Variegata' (Manna grass)
Miscanthus sacchariflorus (Silver banner grass)
Panicum virgatum (Switch grass)
Phalaris arundinacea var. *picta* (Ribbon grass)
Spartina pectinata (Prairie cord grass)
Typha spp. (Cattails)

hold their foliage in a low clump but send up flowering stems that tower above it and obscure all their neighbors in the process — not a good choice for the front of the border unless the stems don't obscure the blooms behind them. Purple moor grass *(Molinia caerulea)*, a low tuft with 4-foot flower stems, can stay up front because its stems are thin and widespread enough to allow a view through them.

Echoing effect

Grasses help to knit a landscape by repeating the form or color of other plants. An echoing effect is easy to produce in both foliage and flower. The loosely mounded hairy melic grass *(Melica ciliata)* looks beautiful beside old shrub roses, especially pink or red floribundas, because its arching spray of pale, whitish flowers mirrors the form of the rose bush. Golden hakonechloa grass *(Hakonechloa macra* 'Aureola') echoes the color of the gold-edged, bold-leaved hosta 'Aureo Marginata'. A more subtle echo can be had by combining a tuft of blue oat grass *(Helictotrichon sempervirens)* or blue fescue *(Festuca glauca)* with the scalloped leaves and nodding blossoms of blue Rocky Mountain columbine. Blue fescue adds texture to any plant with blue-gray leaves.Try it with the gray-blue foliage of cottage pinks and other dianthus, or with steel blue eryngium. For a combination of greens, try a green-flowered zinnia called 'Envy' against the spiky, pale blades of green and white dwarf ribbon grass *(Phalaris arundinacea* 'Dwarf Garters'), a more restrained cultivar of the typical running grass.

Tall grass partners

Perennials of great height usually hail from a prairie heritage, so it's no wonder their looks are improved when they're partnered with grasses. Clusters of madder-purple ironweed *(Vernonia* spp.), golden spikes of compass plant *(Silphium laciniatum)*, and the graceful stems of prairie coneflower *(Ratibida* spp.) are right at home with big bluestem *(Andropogon gerardii)* and switch grass *(Panicum virgatum)*, two grasses that grew with them for eons in the tallgrass prairie. You can translate the effect into other tall plant combinations, too. Try the satiny blooms of red or "black" hollyhock *(Alcea rosea)* with the vivid foliage of red switch grass *(Panicum virgatum* 'Rotstrahlbusch'), for instance.

Grasses with annuals

Annual flowers also look great with grasses. Orange California poppies and meadow grasses like *Stipa* are a natural combination that looks just as good in the garden as in the foothills. Or try russet-colored sunflower 'Autumn Beauty' or the shorter 'Music Box' *(Helianthus annuus)* with tall or mid-height ornamental grasses like sideoats grama *(Bouteloua curtipendula)*, switch grass *(Panicum virgatum)*, or little bluestem *(Schizachyrium scoparium)*.

Annual grasses are in turn excellent with annual flowers or perennials in an informal garden. They add a relaxed look, and because many of them are enthusiastic self-sowers, a meadowlike feel. For the same reasons, you may want to avoid introducing them to a formal perennial border. Hare's tail *(Lagurus ovatus)*, with its fuzzy tufts, adds lighthearted texture to an edging of dwarf or peppermint-striped zinnias. Tall annual grasses with large leaves and architectural form, like ornamental corn varieties, beg for equally outstanding partners such as tall, plumy celosia or the annual amaranth called love-lies-bleeding, which drips with chenille-textured pink flowers.

Grasses with Shrubs

All grasses combine beautifully with deciduous and evergreen shrubs and shrublike plants. Their fine texture against the stouter leaves and branching form of shrubs is always appealing, but never more so than in autumn and winter. The blazing scarlet of sumacs or the crimson-pink of a burning bush is amplified by a nearby planting of frost grass *(Spodiopogon sibiricus)*, whose leaves take on burnished tints of their own in autumn. Later, the spiky texture of the grass shows off against the shrub's bare silhouette. Evergreens reverse the spectacle. In winter they shine against the soft texture and pale color of dormant grasses.

Both clumping and running grasses can be paired with shrubs. Running grasses, such as blue Lyme grass *(Elymus arenarius)*, or self-sowing grasses, such as squirreltail *(Hordeum jubatum)*, can be set free to wander at will among large shrub plantings. With clumping grasses, allow several feet between shrubs and grass plants so they won't have to compete with each other for water and nutrients.

The design considerations discussed previously for combining perennials and grasses can apply to shrubs. Good combinations include contrasting, complementary, or echoing effects. It makes sense to vary the height of a planting, so that tall shrubs are partnered with shorter grasses and vice versa, and to avoid transitions that are too sharp. An extremely tall pampas grass may look awkward with a dwarf azalea. If you'd like to pair the two, adding a third, mid-height plant such as a pennisetum grass or a mugo pine will help make the jump. Low-growing shrubs like heaths and junipers work with mid-height grasses or grasses that grow in mats.

Shrub and grass combinations

Almost any ornamental shrub can be paired with a grass. Here are some good matches:

- Azaleas (*Rhododendron* spp.) with blue fescues *(Festuca glauca)* or plantain-leaved sedge *(Carex plantaginea)*

- Blue spirea *(Caryopteris incana)* with 'Blaze' little bluestem (*Schizachyrium scoparium* 'Blaze')

- Chaste tree *(Vitex agnus-castae)* with porcupine grass (*Miscanthus sinensis* var. *strictus*)

- Deciduous holly *(Ilex verticillata)* with fountain grass (*Pennisetum* spp.) and miscanthus (*Miscanthus* spp.)

- Japanese maples *(Acer palmatum)* with New Zealand hair sedge *(Carex comans)* or other sedges, or beside water with any rushes *(Juncus* spp.)

- Red or golden barberry (*Berberis* spp.) with blue oat grass *(Helictotrichon sempervirens),* blue Lyme grass *(Elymus arenarius),* or blue fescues *(Festuca glauca)*

- Red-twig dogwood *(Cornus stolonifera)* with frost grass *(Spodiopogon sibiricus)*

- Russian sage *(Perovskia atriplicifolia)* or butterfly bush *(Buddleia davidii)* with big bluestem *(Andropogon gerardii)*

- Smoke tree *(Cotinus coggyria)* with 'Yaku Jima' miscanthus, or with 'Sioux Blue' Indian grass (*Sorghastrum nutans* 'Sioux Blue')

- Star magnolia *(Magnolia stellata)* with New Zealand hair sedge *(Carex comans)* or with black-flowered fountain grass (*Pennisetum alopecuroides* 'Moudry')

- Sumacs, especially shining sumac *(Rhus copallina),* with purple top *(Tridens flavus)* or Stipa grasses or little bluestem *(Schizachyrium scoparium)*

- White-stem raspberry *(Rubus cockburnianus)* with Japanese blood grass (*Imperata cylindrica* 'Red Baron') and 'Flamingo' or 'Burgundy Giant' miscanthus

- Witch hazel (*Hamamelis* spp.) with silver banner grass *(Miscanthus sacchariflorus)*

- Yellow-stem dogwood *(Cornus alba)* with perennial quaking grass *(Briza media)*

Grasses in the Shade Garden

Most grasses are sun lovers, so it is surprising that some of the most beautiful ornamentals are at home in the shade. What they lack in size and showy bloom they make up for in stunning form. Colors are generally muted, with plants woven together in a tapestry of greens. Consider the foliage of nearby plants, and then find a texture and color combination that suits your eye.

The most elegant of all grasses, golden hakonechloa (*Hakonechloa macra* 'Aureole') is an exceptional shade grass, offering striking color as well as form. Developed from a forest grass of Japan, it forms a shaggy mound that weeps onto paths and over stones like a narrow-leaved bamboo. Its mane of golden leaves is beautiful with hostas, heucheras, and yellow Welsh poppies *(Meconopsis cambrica),* as well as spring wildflowers and small bulbs. Vivid chartreuse leaves begin emerging about the time that hellebores and brilliant blue Siberian squill *(Scilla sibirica)* and glory-of-the-snow *(Chionodoxa* spp.) come into bloom. For a flourish in autumn, hakonechloa becomes suffused with pink before it dies back for winter.

Another beauty is the ethereal *Deschampsia,* or hair grass, which grows in the wild in lightly wooded areas. Both crinkled hair grass *(D. flexuosa)* and tufted hair grass *(D. caespitosa)* will thrive in light to medium shade in the garden. Tufted hair grass is one of the first ornamental grasses to bloom, and

Grasses for shade

Carex spp. (Sedges)
Chasmanthium latifolium (Wild oats)
Deschampsia caespitosa (Hair grass)
Hakonechloa macra and *H. m.* 'Aureola' (Hakonechloa)
Hystrix patula (Bottlebrush grass)
Imperata cylindrica 'Red Baron' (Japanese blood grass)
Luzula nivea 'Snowbird' ('Snowbird' snowy wood rush)
Milium effusum 'Aureum' (Golden wood millet)
Panicum clandestinum (Deer tongue grass)
Sasa palmata (Running bamboo)
Sasa veitchii (Silver-edge bamboo)
Sorghastrum nutans (Indian grass)
Spodiopogon sibericus (Frost grass)
Tridens flavus (Purple top)

its cloud of delicate panicles almost glows in the company o
ferns and hostas.

The interesting grass known as bottlebrush *(Hystrix patula,*
is a woodsy annual with bristly seed heads that look just like
a slender bottlebrush. This grass is a good one to start in a
naturalistic woodland garden, where it can self-sow with small
black-eyed Susan *(Rudbeckia triloba),* blue American bellflower *(Campanula americana),* and other shade-loving, summer-blooming wildflowers. No matter where you first plant
it, bottlebrush will tend to gravitate to a place of honor along
paths and openings where the panicles can catch the light
Children can't resist stroking its fully mature seed heads just
to watch how easily they shatter.

Screening with Grass

When you want to hide a view of the street, your neighbor's
RV, or the compost pile, you can install tall ornamental
grasses for a fast-growing screen. Miscanthus and pampas
grasses are popular choices for a screen, thanks to their great
height and dense foliage. These grasses will give you good coverage in as little as two years from container-grown plants.You
can mix and match for an informal screen, plant a single cultivar for a more conservative look, or intersperse variegated
cultivars among green grasses for something different. Even a
single plant of the variegated pampas grass known as 'Silver
Comet' *(Cortaderia selloana* 'Silver Comet') will add interest
to a plain green hedge.

An impenetrable hedge can be made of prairie cord grass
(Spartina pectinata). Reaching 6 feet high, it has unfriendly
razor-sharp leaf edges that discourage all who try to cross it

Grasses for screening
Arundo donax (Giant reed)
Bambusa oldhamii (Giant timber bamboo)
Calamagrostis acutiflora (Feather reed grass)
Cortaderia selloana (Pampas grass)
Erianthus ravennae (Ravenna grass)
Miscanthus, tall cultivars
Panicum virgatum, tall cultivars (Switch grass)
Phyllostachys aureosulcata (Yellow groove bamboo)
Phyllostachys nigra (Black bamboo)
Pleioblastus viridistratus (Golden bamboo)
Semiarundinaria murielae (Running bamboo)

path. You'll be able to block traffic from short-cutters or straying pets and enjoy rich yellow color in fall. Consider carefully before you plant — cord grass can spread aggressively, and it's no fun to try to remove. Corral the spread by installing a foot-deep barrier of plastic or galvanized metal at planting time, and be alert for escapees, which are easier to root out when young.

For year-round screening, turn to bamboo. Other grasses will have to be cut down in spring to allow room for new growth, so you'll be without a screen until the grass reaches full height in summer. Some hardy bamboos may shed their leaves in winter, but the stems will still have a screening effect. Yellow groove bamboo *(Phyllostachys aureosulcata)* and other semievergreen types hang on to their foliage through much of the winter. Black bamboo *(Phyllostachys nigra)*, with its unique glossy black stems, makes a spectacular screen, or a gorgeous addition to a screen of mixed grasses. Like yellow-groove and black bamboo, many bamboos are determined ramblers, and new shoots can spring up yards away from the parent plant. Don't plant them unless you have lots of space to sacrifice or you can install a deep, impenetrable barrier at planting time.

Ground Covers

Ornamental grasses, like their turf-grass cousins, make superb ground covers. Whether short or tall, clump-forming or running, any grass that spreads well can be an effective cover. The old favorite known as ribbon grass or gardener's garters *(Phalaris arundinacea* var. *picta)*, as well as tufted hair grass *(Deschampsia caespitosa)* and the beautiful blue Lyme grass

Grasses as ground covers

Carex plantaginea (Plantain-leaved sedge)
Carex texensis (Catlin sedge)
Deschampsia caespitosa (Tufted hair grass)
Elymus arenarius (Blue Lyme grass)
Festuca amethystina (Sheep's fescue)
Festuca glauca, species and cultivars (Blue fescue)
Koelreria macrantha (June grass)
Miscanthus sacchariflorus (Silver banner grass)
Phalaris arundinacea var. *picta* (Ribbon grass)
Sasa palmata (Running bamboo)
Sasa veitchii (Silver-edge bamboo)

(Elymus arenarius), are good mid-height ground covers. They combine well with ground-hugging junipers and heathers, or with red-berried cotoneaster. In a shady garden, clumps of plantain-leaved sedge *(Carex plantaginea)* provide a handsome ground cover.

Tall grasses and bamboos can also be used as ground covers, making an appealing grove of rustling foliage. *Sasa palmata* is a little tall for what we usually think of as a ground cover, reaching 6 feet or more in height, but it spreads rapidly by underground runners and fills in fast in shade or sun. This attractive bamboo has solid green leaves that spread wide like an open palm. Similar in shape but not in color are the striking white-edged leaves of *Sasa veitchii*, a smaller running bamboo that lights up shady spots.

If you're tired of mowing, consider substituting a naturally low-growing grass in parts of your lawn. Buffalo grass *(Buchloe dactyloides)* spreads by runners to create a thick, low turf. Several cultivars have been developed for western states because of their lawn-grass potential. One drawback is that the spiny seed husks can cling to pets and socks. Blue grama *(Bouteloua gracilis)*, another naturally low-growing species is also getting attention as a low-maintenance lawn grass in the dry West.

A steep slope planted with ornamental grasses is much easier to care for and much more pleasing to the eye than one covered with turf grass. Both clumping and running types make excellent covers for slopes because their fibrous roots knit together to secure the soil. Running grasses will spread naturally to cover the area, but you can create the same effect by planting clumping grasses tightly together. June grass *(Koelreria macrantha)* is good for dry slopes.

A single mass planting of pennisetum is lovely on slopes, their arched foliage giving the impression of a waterfall. Mixed plantings provide more interest. The filmy white plumes of the spreading *Miscanthus sacchariflorus* make a striking early autumn combination with the warm chestnut-orange of little bluestem and the tawny gold of switch grass For a low-maintenance slope that looks good all year, combine warm-season and cool-season grasses. The latter will be greening up as the former die down. Mixing warm-season grasses with evergreens, such as ground-cover junipers or heathers and heaths, will also add contrasting color and texture through all the seasons.

Meadow, Prairie, and Wildlife Plantings

Grasses are right where they belong in meadows and prairies In spring and summer, native grasses are the canvas for the

Grasses for a naturalistic planting

Andropogon gerardii (Big bluestem)
Aristidia purpurea (Purple three-awn)
Bouteloua spp. (Grama grasses)
Eragrostis spectabilis (Purple love grass)
Erianthus ravennae (Ravenna grass)
Hordeum jubatum (Squirreltail grass)
Muhlenbergia filipes (Purple muhly)
Panicum virgatum (Switch grass)
Schizachyrium scoparium (Little bluestem)
Sorghastrum nutans (Indian grass)
Sporobolus heterolepsis (Prairie dropseed)
Stipa spp.
Tridens flavus (Purple top)

bright strokes of wildflower color, and when the flower show is over, grasses keep our attention with ripening seed heads and bright winter foliage. The plants on the list of grasses for naturalistic plantings are wilder-looking selections than the clumps recommended for accents or eye-catchers elsewhere. They'll offer good cover, a banquet of food, and a source of nesting material for birds, small mammals, and a host of other wild creatures.

Water Gardens and Wet Sites

A reflection in still water doubles the pleasure of a grass planting. Giant cane *(Arundo donax)* may seem out of place in the middle of a front lawn but is perfectly at ease at the edge of a large pool, its strongly vertical foliage providing pleasing contrast to the rounded leaves of other water plants, like lotus, lilies, and blue-flowered pickerelweed. *Miscanthus sinensis* cultivars are popular choices for the edges of smaller pools, creating rippling fountains of greenery that echo the ebb and flow of water. Mounded grasses such as fountain grass (*Pennisetum* spp.) and leather-leaf sedge *(Carex buchananii)* trail their leaf tips on the liquid surface of ponds, blurring the boundary between land and water. Upright grasses such as 'Karl Foerster' feather reed grass (*Calamagrostis acutiflora* 'Karl Foerster') add a formal touch to small pools edged in stone.

Grasses grown at the edge of man-made ponds don't necessarily find themselves in wet soil, but some grasses don't mind getting their feet wet and are good candidates for poorly

Grasses for water gardens and wet sites

Grasses that will grow in average garden conditions as well as wet or boggy soil are indicated by an asterisk. All others will grow in boggy soil or standing shallow water.

* *Acorus* spp. (Sweet flag)

   Calamagrostis acutiflora (Feather reed grass)

   Cyperus spp. (Papyrus)

* *Equisetum* spp. (Horsetail)

   Eriophorum latifolium (Cotton grass)

* *Glyceria* spp. (Manna grass)

   Juncus, all spp. and cultivars (Rushes)

   Schoenplectus lacustris ssp. *tabernaemontani* 'Zebrinus' (Banded bulrush)

   Scirpus cernuus (Low bulrush)

* *Spartina pectinata* (Prairie cord grass)

   Typha spp. (Cattails)

drained sites. Variegated manna grass (*Glyceria maxima* 'Variegata') will spread from dry land right out into the water. Feather reed grass *(Calamagrostis acutiflora)* adapts well to life in the muck. If you bring cattails (*Typha* spp.) into the water garden you'll admire their good vertical line and get a close look at the fascinating life cycle of their flowers. You may also get to see songbirds collecting the cattail fluff to line a cozy nest. Horsetails and rushes are other grasslike plants for water gardens and wet sites.

One of the most charming grasses for a wet site is cotton grass *(Eriophorum latifolium),* which sprouts furry white puffs in bloom, as if someone scattered a bag of cotton balls in the garden. This grass will grow right in water and looks great backed by purple or blue Japanese iris. Razor-sharp cord grass *(Spartina pectinata)* will flourish in a wet spot, but be sure to plant it well away from walks or swingsets.

A wet site can be home to a fabulous array of rushes (*Juncus* spp.). Soft rush *(Juncus effusus)* will sometimes show up on its own, brought in by birds' feet or sprouted from long-dormant seed. Its soft brown flowers dangle from the tips of the stems in an outward-arching burst of slim, dark foliage. Australian silver rush *(Juncus polyanthemos)* is a tall plant with delicately thin leaves that stretch to 4 feet tall. The spires of red cardinal flower make a brilliant accent against the soft blue-gray foliage of this rush. California gray rush *(Juncus patens)* is similar but stands at attention. The horizontally striped leaves of banded bulrush *(Schoenplectus tabernae-montana* 'Zebrinus') create a sun-dappled effect in a water or bog garden.

If you want to try some moisture-loving plants, but nature hasn't provided you with a wet spot, you can make your own by burying a child's preformed plastic swimming pool and filling it with soil. The plastic lining makes it easy to control the moisture in the soil to create a bog garden. A plastic bucket works on a smaller scale. On the patio, you can grow plants such as papyrus (*Cyperus* spp.), whose roots need to be in water, by planting in a clay pot, then placing the pot inside a plastic bucket and keeping the bucket filled with water.

Grasses for Xeriscaping and Dry Sites

Drought-tolerant grasses are increasingly in demand as homeowners become more aware of the need to conserve water. They include cool-season grasses that evolved where a dose of winter or spring rainfall is followed by months of dryness and warm-season grasses from the prairies, whose extensive root systems make the most of limited rainfall. Many of these drought-tolerant plants are clump-forming rather than running grasses, each clump claiming a territory from which its spreading roots draw reserves of water. If you live in a dry climate, remember to keep fire safety in mind when planting grasses near the house, particularly cool-season grasses, which dry out in the summer.

Drought-tolerant grasses do more than just survive dry conditions. The cool-season *Stipa* grasses are beautiful, shimmering plants. Purple three-awn *(Aristida purpurea)*, a native of the dry Southwest, is a beautiful grass to combine with native wildflowers such as desert marigold and globe mallow. It has filmy, gray-green foliage and panicles with long, silken hairs that catch the light. Another gardenworthy western native is Indian rice grass *(Oryzopsis hymenoides)*, whose wiry sprays of seed heads bring birds to the garden. By June it acquires a golden straw color that lights up a naturalistic planting. Drought-tolerant junipers make the perfect backdrop.

Grasses that evolved on the prairies often have huge root systems and do well in gardens where rainfall is scant because of huge root systems. Plants like Indian grass *(Sorghastrum nutans)* and big bluestem *(Andropogon gerardii)* are good tall-grass species for dry gardens. Shortgrass prairie types, such as buffalo grass and blue grama *(Bouteloua gracilis)*, though sometimes only 4 inches tall, have root systems that may reach

Grasses for dry sites

Andropogon gerardii (Big bluestem)
Aristida purpurea (Purple three-awn)
Bouteloua spp. (Grama grasses)
Buchloe dactyloides (Buffalo reed grass)
Dasylirion texanum (Sotol)
Deschampsia spp. (Hair grass)
Eragrostis spp. (Love grass)
Festuca gautieri (Bearskin fescue)
Festuca glauca (Blue fescue)
Koeleria macrantha (Crested hair grass)
Muhlenbergia spp. (Muhly grass)
Oryzopsis hymenoides (Indian rice grass)
Pennisetum spp. (Fountain grass)
Poa compressa (Australian blue grass)
Sorghastrum nutans (Indian grass)
Stipa spp. (Feather grasses)
Yucca filamentosa (Adam's needle)

4 feet long. All the grama grasses flourish in dry gardens. Side-oats grama *(Bouteloua curtipendula)* naturalizes easily with native wildflowers and is appealing with gray-leaved artemisias. Its seeds dangle like a row of little bells from only one side of the stem.

Growing Ornamental Grasses

If all plants were as easy to grow as grasses, we'd have little excuse to putter around the garden. They adapt to a wide range of climates and soils, need little or no maintenance, and resist almost all pests and diseases. A grass chosen with the conditions of your garden in mind will reward you with many years of unfailing good health and good looks and require almost nothing in return.

Choose Wisely

Although adaptability is one of grass's strongest points, selecting a grass with your climate, soil, and sun or shade conditions in mind is important if you want your plant to grow its best. As you read the following general suggestions on selection, keep in mind that the encyclopedia provides specific requirements of the grasses in this book.

Many of the most popular grasses will tolerate minimum temperatures found in much of the continental United States. These grasses are likely to die back in cold-winter climates and stay evergreen where winters are mild. Striped giant reed, for example, is evergreen in Zones 8 to 10 but freezes to beige in climates below Zone 8 before it regrows in spring. Hardiness zones indicate only the lowest temperatures a plant can survive. For some grasses, the quality of summer heat is a more important factor than minimum temperatures. Many will thrive in hot, dry summers but languish in humidity. Others need moist summer air to flourish.

Most, but not all, grasses prefer full sun. Sun lovers like prairie dropseed (*Sporobolus heterolepsis*) flop sadly in shade. Crinkled hair grass (*Deschampsia flexuosa*), on the other hand, thrives in cool, dim light. Ornamental grasses are adaptable to a wide range of soils, some thriving equally well in sand, clay, or perfect loam. Many perform best in average garden soil but will tolerate adverse conditions. Sedges and rushes, for example, will tolerate average garden conditions, but generally grow taller and more robust in wet soils. As mentioned in the previous chapter, the rich soil of a garden bed can be more problematic than poor soil, inducing too much growth and producing floppy plants.

A good way to ensure that your plants are a match for your climate and conditions is to grow species native to your region. They can be just as beautiful as those developed by breeders or brought from overseas. Visit sites in the wild similar to those you have or wish to create on your property and see what grows there. With the landowner's permission, you might bring home a plant. Otherwise, order from one of the steadily increasing number of suppliers specializing in native plants.

Maintenance isn't much of a factor in selecting grasses. Most require little maintenance to look good and less to stay healthy. In fact, most grasses need attention only once a year, when old foliage is removed from dormant plants to make way for new growth. (You might even dispense with that; in the wild, of course, new growth comes right up through the old.) If you are growing cool-season grasses in a border, you may want to remove dormant foliage earlier if it detracts from nearby plants making a show during the summer and fall. Some grasses, such as variegated Japanese silver grass (*Miscanthus sinensis* 'Variegatus'), spill over under their own weight. This can be a beautiful effect along a fence, but where a stiffer backbone is required, be prepared to cut off the flopped foliage and let the plant regrow from the roots, which it will do in a few weeks.

Selecting for fire safety

Dry grasses make excellent tinder, a danger for gardeners in the West, where fires are a natural part of the ecological cycle. Fire-safety guidelines for landscaping call for plants that provide a minimum amount of potential fuel. A giant clump of miscanthus feeds a fire much better than a low tuft of fescue. Cool-season grasses are often dry and dormant during brushfire season. If fire is a problem in your area, avoid summer-dormant grasses such as *Stipa* varieties, and cut back the foliage of any grasses you grow to 4 inches as soon as it ripens.

Safety guidelines for fire-prone areas recommend that 30 feet separate your house from vegetation, and many landscapers discourage planting grasses within 70 feet of the house. Outside this buffer zone, plantings of perennials, shrubs, and grasses should be staggered into self-contained, well-separated island beds. A low hedge of ornamental grass weaving through your garden is a red-carpet route that flames will follow to your door.

Invasive plants and noxious weed

Planting a rampant growing grass can initiate a life-long struggle, and these plants are usually best avoided. But some invasive grasses have their uses. Their wantonness can be an asset in naturalized plantings like meadows and prairies, or where a quick ground cover is needed. Even so, it is foolhardy to plant invasive grasses that offer no methods of control. Some can be reined in by in-ground barriers that impede the spread of rhizomes or stolons. Those that spread by seed may be restricted by cold winters, which kill the seed, or by mulching or hand weeding. Adverse soil conditions or the proximity of strong, competitive plants can retard some otherwise rampant grasses, such as blue Lyme grass (*Elymus arenarius* 'Glaucus').

A few invasive grasses have escaped the confines of gardens and fields to become bona fide pests. Readers in the South and West will be familiar with Johnson grass, introduced in the 1830s for its promise as a superior hay crop and now a noxious headache. While we haven't included noxious weeds in this book, some grasses that behave respectably in certain conditions become problems in others. The African grasses known as feathertop (*Pennisetum villosum*) and natal grass (*Rhychelytrum repens*) are well behaved in cold climates where their seeds aren't viable. In warm climates, however, they self-seed prolifically and should be avoided. If you have any doubt about a grass you're planting, consult a local nursery or extension agent.

Acquiring Grasses

As noted in the first chapter, most garden centers stock at least a few of the most popular grasses, such as miscanthus, blue fescues, pampas grass, and fountain grass. Versatile, beautiful, and easy to grow, these selections are perfect for beginners. Fortunate readers may live near a nursery specializing in grasses, where you can see a wider range of grasses before making your choices. For the widest selection of grasses, consult the list of specialty mail-order nurseries in the back of this book.

Gardeners like to pass along samples of their favorite plants to friends and family. This can be a boon to your garden and pocketbook, but be wary. Like perennials, the grasses you get over the gate are probably the most rampant growers in the garden, with wandering roots. That's how they multiply fast enough to provide divisions to pass along. The root masses of more self-contained clumping species usually knit together into an impenetrable whole that requires the vigorous use of an axe to hack off divisions. Even a favorite neighbor probably won't go to that length to hand you a sample (though you may be handed the axe).

The grasses you buy at garden centers and from some mail-order suppliers will be potted in containers. Buying plants in containers is a great idea for busy gardeners. The plants can sit in their pots for weeks or even months without damage, until you have a chance to set them into the garden. All you have to do is water them. You'll have a choice between very young plants in containers as small as 4 inches across or mature landscape-ready specimens in huge plastic tubs. Before you succumb to the instant gratification of big plants, consider that grasses grow rapidly to full size. If you can wait a year or two, your young plant will catch up to the much more expensive older specimen.

Most mail-order nurseries ship their plants bare-root. Sent while dormant, these plants arrive unpotted, with a small ball of soil or some moisture-retaining material around the roots. First-time mail-order buyers are often dismayed when their first purchases arrive. A spindly plant of switch grass may show only a few stems of leaves, yet its roots may dangle a foot long and in such a thick bunch you can't get your hand around them. Remember that the plant is dormant and that grasses put their effort into growing far-reaching roots before their tops begin to flourish.

Bare-root plants should be planted as soon as possible. Specify an arrival date that suits your schedule, or have the plants delivered to your place of business so they don't sit on a sunny doorstep for hours waiting for you to get home from

Grasses to grow from seed

These grasses are especially easy to grow from seed.

Bouteloua curtipendula

Bouteloua gracilis

Briza media

Coix lacryma-jobi

Eragrostis curvula

Eragrostis spectabilis

Eragrostis trichoides 'Bend'

Erianthus ravennae

Hordeum jubatum

Hystrix patula

Koeleria spp.

Lagurus ovatus

Melica spp.

Oryzopsis milliacea

Panicum spp.

Pennisetum setaceum

Pennisetum villosum

Rhychelytrum repens

Sorghastrum nutans

Stipa spp.

Tridens falvus

Tripsicum dactyloides

Zea mays

work. Unpack the plants right away and inspect the roots. If they're dried out, broken, rotted, or diseased, call the supplier (reputable firms will replace damaged plants). If the plant looks healthy and you just need a few hours to prepare a planting hole, wrap the roots in very moist paper towels or pop them in a bucket of water. If you haven't decided on a permanent home for the plants, set each one into a good-sized pot of soil and water it in well. Then you can transplant when you're ready, in a week or a month.

Growing ornamental grasses from seed is inexpensive and fun, and every year it seems catalogs offer more choices. (Annual grasses are sometimes listed under "everlastings" in catalogs.) Remember, however, that a plant grown from seed may not reproduce the exact traits of its parents, which is why most ornamental grasses are propagated by division. Blue Lyme grass *(Elymus arenarius),* for example, is fairly easy to start from seed, but the seedlings may range from green to gray to steel blue in color. Some plants set infertile seed; others are slow to germinate or slow to reach mature size from seed. The list above includes good selections to grow from seed.

When to plant

Warm-season grasses do best if planted in early spring so they become established before the punishing heat of summer. If you transplant in summer, be generous with the watering hose and rig up some temporary shade for new plants for the first couple of weeks. Except in mild-winter areas, fall planting is unwise because it generally doesn't allow time for roots to establish themselves enough to resist being heaved out of the ground during freeze-thaw cycles. A thick blanket of mulch or a constant cover of deep snow may help insulate the soil and the crown of the plant enough to carry it through the winter, but why chance it. Cool-season grasses can be placed in the ground in spring, summer, or fall. If you plant in fall, be aware that the aboveground portion of the grass may not come to life until late winter or early spring; but the unseen roots will be busy settling in.

Preparing a Site for Planting

Not the least of the attractions of ornamental grasses is the ease with which they can be planted. You seldom have to improve the drainage, fertility, or tilth of your soil before planting, particularly if you've chosen grasses adapted to your climate and soil conditions. New beds and borders or larger plantings such as meadows and prairies will take some muscle power, but mainly to remove turf or weeds. (You can even plant clumping types directly into existing vegetation without clearing or tilling the soil.) You can choose among the following methods for clearing a new planting bed based on the size of the bed, the type of vegetation to remove, and the amount of time you can invest.

Stripping off existing turf

For mixed beds or borders where lawn now grows, you can remove the turf by either hand or machine. With a sharp spade, you can remove sod from a 5-foot by 20-foot bed in an afternoon. Rent a power sod cutter (available from most home and garden rental businesses) for larger areas. The machine, which peels long strips of sod about 18 inches wide, is about as easy to handle as a rotary tiller.

To strip sod by hand, first remove tap-rooted weeds such as dandelions, dock, or Queen-Anne's-lace. (Do this before power stripping, too.) Outline a strip of turf about 18 inches wide and 3 feet to 4 feet long by making vertical cuts 3 inches to 4 inches deep with a flat spade. Working in from the edges of the strip, slice horizontally through the roots. Roll the loosened strip backward upon itself, exactly as you would roll up a rug. Keep your dandelion digger handy to free clinging roots. Repeat the procedure as needed. You can transplant the turflike sod or cut it into smaller pieces, shake out loose soil onto the planting bed, then compost the remainder. Turn the pieces upside down so that the grass dies and rots.

Smothering vegetation

A slower but less laborious method than stripping sod, smothering vegetation blocks air and sunlight to kill grass and weeds. Use sheets of black plastic, thick overlapping sections of newspaper, or an 8- to 10-inch layer of dense mulch such as clean straw, grass clippings, or chopped leaves. Smothering a bed can take much longer than stripping sod, up to several months. During a hot summer, however, a plastic mulch can kill vegetation in less than a week.

A combination of stripping and smothering will work well if you're planting a bed of widely spaced ornamental grasses. Strip the sod from the immediate planting areas around the grasses, then smother the rest of the bed with newspaper topped by a deep layer of organic mulch.

Cultivation

Tilling under unwanted vegetation with a rotary or tractor tiller will kill many existing plants. Repeat the tilling at least three times, about a week apart, to kill survivors and seedlings that will germinate from dormant seeds brought to life by disturbing the site. Tilling is not a good method for sites infested with quack grass, Bermuda grass, Johnson grass, or other rhizomatous plants whose severed rhizomes will quickly produce new plants.

Chemical eradication

For large-scale plantings, such as meadow or prairie gardens, the most practical solution may be to apply a glyphosate-based herbicide, sold as Roundup, Kleenup, or Ranger. Highly toxic, these compounds kill all types of vegetation on the site, but break down completely in a relatively short period after application. (Organic gardeners can use the methods above to clear and plant small parts of the larger area, until eventually the whole site is planted.) Apply exactly as the label directs on a windless day, and expect the vegetation to begin turning brown in about 10 days. Wait several weeks to see if weeds reappear and warrant another application. Herbicides are effective against quack and Bermuda grass infestations, but the tenacious Johnson grass has been known to resist even agricultural-strength chemical assassins.

Soil amendments

Some of the grasses you want to grow may require improvements in your soil's fertility or drainage. With grasses, it's best not to be too generous, which encourages rapid, weaker growth. But digging in an inch or two of compost or aged manure at planting time will reward you with lush, healthy young plants that quickly make a splash in the garden. These immature grasses will fill in more quickly if their roots can pull in liberal amounts of nutrients.

In areas of clay soil, where water is likely to collect in wintertime, you can improve drainage by working in liberal amounts of sand and compost before planting. (Be aware that adding too little sand to heavy clay can produce concretelike soil.) These amendments will also raise the area of your planting bed above the surrounding soil, creating a mounded bed effect that helps water drain away from the rot-vulnerable crowns of the plants.

Planting

Dig a hole, plop in a plant, fill in the hole, water, and presto. Although planting is a simple process, we offer the following pointers to help ensure a successful and appealing result.

Spacing

Adequate elbow room is important for the looks and health of any plant. Clumping grasses have such distinctive forms that most are best appreciated when they have room to breathe. Crowded plants are also more susceptible to fungal disease. A general rule of thumb is to base the spacing on the mature height of the plant — if a miscanthus reaches 4 feet tall, plant the next specimen 4 feet away, measuring from the center of one plant to the center of the next. Spacing is not a science. Some gardeners allow a little extra room, while others prefer the look of plants that overlap and flow upon one another. In addition to considering space between plants, you should consider space between plants and people. Hanging into walkways or paths, grass blades can be annoying ticklers or downright dangerous if they possess sharp-edged leaves.

Planting container-grown and bare-root grasses

It's easy to plant container-grown plants. Dig a hole big enough to accommodate the root ball, fill it with water, and let the water soak into the surrounding soil. Turn the pot upside down with your hand across the top, slip the plant out, and put the root ball into the hole. Fill the hole with soil, firm it into place, and water the plant thoroughly with a gentle spray or slow trickle. This technique works for planting into a prepared bed or for planting a specimen in the lawn or other existing vegetation.

If roots encircle the ball of soil, gently untangle them and spread them out in the planting hole. Make sure the crown of the plant sits in the hole at the same depth as in the pot or a little higher than the surrounding soil. If you bury the crown too deeply the shoots may not have enough strength

Planting Timetable

Sow seeds in pots	Spring or summer
Sow seeds in garden	Early spring
Sow cool-season grasses	Fall, in mild-winter climates
Plant bare-root warm-season grasses	Early spring, or year-round in mild climates
Plant container-grown grasses	Early spring or summer, or year-round in mild climates
Plant container-grown or bare-root cool-season grasses	Spring or early fall

to fight their way to the surface and the depression in the soil will trap water around the crown and cause rot. If you miscalculated on the depth of the hole, lift the plant out (slide your hand under the root ball, don't grab the foliage or crown), and add and firm soil in the hole until you reach the necessary height. Firm it down before final planting so it doesn't settle excessively later.

After watering in the new transplant, you can spread a thin layer of compost or aged manure over the soil surface around the plant, to a distance of 8 to 10 inches from the crown, but the extra nutrients aren't really necessary. To help retain moisture, mulch very young plants with an inch or two of grass clippings or other organic matter, and older transplants (from gallon pots) with 2 to 3 inches of organic material. Keep the crown of the plant free of mulch.

Plant bare-root grasses in much the same way as container plants, as soon as possible after they arrive. Trim off dead or damaged roots, then support the plant in the hole with one hand as you work soil around the roots with the other. Make sure the crown is at the level of the surrounding soil or slightly above.

Direct seeding

Some annual grasses are quick to sprout and can be sown directly in a bed or border like a pack of marigolds. Following the timetable and depth directions on the seed packet, simply sprinkle the seeds onto bare, loosened soil and keep them

moist until germination. Watch for competing weeds that may
arise, and snip them off with manicure scissors at the base, to
avoid disturbing the grass roots. Hare's tail *(Lagurus ovatus)*
is an excellent grass to sow directly into the border. The en-
dearing fuzzy heads are charming in a mixed planting of
flowers and grasses. Tender fountain grass *(Pennisetum setaceum),* which is treated as an annual in cold-winter climates,
is another rewarding grass to seed in place. (We'll discuss how
to seed a large area, such as a meadow or prairie, later in the
chapter.)

Planting seeds in pots

Perennial grasses are best sown in pots, then transplanted
into the garden. Not only do many perennials take longer than
annuals to germinate, the little plants are easy to lose track
of in the garden. The techniques are much the same as the
ones you use to start vegetables or perennials from seed. Consult the packet for any special requirements (some seeds need
to be refrigerated, for example). Sow two to four seeds in a
3- or 4-inch plastic pot or a deep, skinny pot or cell-pack that
allows the roots to extend downward naturally instead of coiling around the walls. Keep the seeds moist until germination,
then place the little seedlings under lights or in a bright window. Unlike vegetables or perennials which need to be thinned
to only one plant in the pot, all of these little grass plants
may be left to form a clump.

When the seedlings are several inches tall, harden them off
before planting in the garden, just as you would annual or
perennial flower seedlings. This process involves exposing the
plant to outdoor conditions away from the wind a little at a
time over several weeks, at first for an hour, then for a couple of hours, then half a day, then all day, then finally for several days. You'll usually notice a visible change in color and
texture as the grass leaves toughen up to meet outdoor conditions. Fertilizer should be cut back about two weeks before
you move the plants outside, then stopped altogether in the
last week or several days.

Planting on a slope

Instead of stripping away existing vegetation and exposing
soil to erosion from rain and wind, you can smother unwanted plants on a slope with a thick layer of newspaper or
mulch and plant container-grown grasses through the mulch.
The old vegetation holds the soil but doesn't compete for
water or nutrients while the new grasses become established.
If you must strip away old vegetation, spread a heavy organic
mulch (about 4 inches thick) and plant through it as soon as

ossible. You'll need about 1 cubic yard of mulch to cover 100 quare feet to that depth.

Start planting at the top of the slope, setting plants more losely together than you would in a border to prevent dam-ge from erosion. Build up soil on the down-slope side of each lanting hole so you can place the plant's crown level, instead f following the slope's incline. On steep slopes, push a vooden shingle into the soil or nestle a stone on the down-lope side to prevent the soil from washing away before the oots take hold. As a further erosion-control measure, drip rrigate the plants. If you don't have a drip hose, set a plastic nilk jug next to each plant, and poke a small hole in the bot-om to release water slowly into the soil.

The techniques described later in the chapter for direct-eeding a meadow or prairie will also work for a slope, just ake extra care with mulching and watering to avoid erosion.

Planting in boggy soil or water

Installing plants in ponds or wet, boggy soil will take you back to the days when you played in puddles or made mud ies. The task is as simple and as messy. For a large boggy rea, old clothes are advisable, along with a pair of high rub-er boots and two squares of plywood large enough to sup-ort your weight. A 2-foot square should support up to 150 ounds, a 3-foot square anyone heavier. You can use them like tepping stones as you move through the wet soil, using a ong-handled hoe to move one square out of the muck while ou stand on the other.

To plant, scoop out a hole big enough for the roots or root all and refill it with the muck you removed. Placing the rown is not critical, because the water level of bogs and wet-ands fluctuates, but don't bury the plant. You needn't bother vith mulch or additional watering, unless you're in the mid-lle of a prolonged dry spell.

For true water plants, such as papyrus (*Cyperus* spp.), work ander water and plant into the pond bottom, if you have a oil-bottomed pond and the plants are hardy in your area. If ou have a lined pond or the plants aren't hardy, plant in pots. Keeping the plants in pots makes them easy to remove both or storage in winter and when the pool needs maintenance. uppliers selling water plants can often provide detailed in-tructions for planting and care. In general, common water plants will do well planted in plastic or terra cotta pots filled vith heavy loam garden soil and fertilized periodically with pecial pellets. Cover the soil surface with coarse gravel to old the soil in place under water. Be sure to plant or set the pots at the water depth recommended for the plant.

Establishing a prairie or meadow

The allure of a broad expanse of wildflowers and grasse dotted with birds and butterflies, has fueled the popularity "meadow in a can" gardens. Unfortunately, most of these e forts end in failure — establishing a sustainable meadow prairie planting is a lot of work. Before setting out to conve a large swath of property to meadow or prairie, weigh the e fort with the reward. You may decide that growing wild flowers and grasses in the more controlled confines of one more smaller beds or borders makes more sense. We'll ou line the procedures for making a meadow or prairie plantin here. It is a good idea to consult with a local wildflower e pert (try your nursery or extension agent) to determine th best mix of plants for your area and to find out what meth ods of installation, care, and maintenance have proven mo successful in local conditions.

Unless you have the money to buy large quantities of co tainer-grown plants, or the time and space to start them fro seed, you'll need to direct-seed the site. (Small sites can b planted with transplants or plugs and the bare soil heavil mulched to control weeds.) Sow meadow and prairie grasse in late spring or early summer in cold climates. Most of the are warm-season plants, germinating best when soil heats u in spring. If you live in an area prone to summer drough move the planting schedule up a few weeks. Seed in the fa in mild-winter areas where the soil stays warm year-round an rainfall is abundant following planting.

Eliminating the competitive existing vegetation is the firs step to a successful meadow or prairie planting. Any of th techniques described earlier in the chapter will work, thoug for larger areas tilling or chemical eradication may be the mos practical. These methods eliminate plants, but weed seeds wi still lie in wait by the millions, ready to spring into action a soon as you till the soil. Wait a week to 10 days after tillin or cultivating the soil, and lightly hoe off any weeds tha sprout. Repeat this procedure once or twice.

Once cleared, small areas can be sowed the old-fashione way, by hand, or with a lawn-grass or fertilizer spreade Larger areas will require a tractor; you might even want t hire a farmer with a mechanical seed drill. Seed quantitie will vary depending on the mix of wildflowers and grasses yo choose. In general, an acre of grasses would require 10 pound of seed, or 1 pound per thousand square feet. Prepare the see by mixing it with an extender, such as vermiculite, sand, saw dust, or Kitty Litter, so that it will be easy to see what area you've already covered. Combine about 4 pounds of Kitty Lit ter or sand with every pound of seed. If you use dry vermi culite or sawdust, use about a 5-gallon bucketful for each half ound of seed, and dampen the mix slightly so that the seed sticks to the extender and doesn't sift to the bottom of the bucket.

To broadcast seed by hand, scatter it with steady, even tosses. To ensure good coverage, walk and sow in parallel rows, then repeat, walking perpendicular to your first passes. After scattering the seed, rake the area lightly, so that about a quarter-inch of soil covers the seed. For a big area, wire a piece of chain-link fence fabric or stock fence behind a garden tractor and pull it across the field. Grass seeds sprout best when they're pressed firmly into the soil. A water-filled lawn roller (rented locally) is easy to handle, because you can fill it to a weight that you can manage. If you're planting a big sweep of grasses, hitch up a roller attachment to the tractor that tilled your field and go over the area thoroughly. After rolling the planted area, scatter a light covering of clean wheat or oat straw across it. Shake out any clumps so you don't impede the growth of seedling grasses. Set up overhead sprinklers and water at least an inch. To measure the amount of water, set out empty cat food or tuna cans at various places.

Water an additional quarter-inch to half-inch (depending on your weather) every other day, so that the top layer of soil stays moist and hospitable to emerging roots. You'll see green shoots within days after planting, but your new planting won't look much like a lawn. These grasses will be putting their energy into root growth, not top growth. Leave the straw in place to naturally decompose, but watch for emerging broadleaf weeds and remove the most rampant growers. Your grasses won't be able to keep pace with fast-growing annual weeds, and you'll find it impossible to weed the whole area. So, when the weeds reach about 8 inches high, mow with the blade set at about 4 inches, to knock the weeds back and let sunlight reach the seedling grasses. When the weeds regrow to that 8-inch height, check the height of your grass seedlings, then set the mower accordingly and mow again. Those fast-growing weeds are annuals, and it may take three mowings or more the first season to knock them down to size.

If your new meadow or prairie includes wildflowers as well as grasses, you'll have to depend on hand-pulling the worst of the weeds until your flowers bloom and set seed. A mowing before then would knock the wildflowers back (particularly fast-growing annuals) and probably kill off quite a few. Once the wildflowers have set seed, mowing the meadow will bring light to young grasses and help to scatter the flower seeds. Check the height of your grasses and set the mower just above them. As a bonus, some of your flowers may put forth another round of bloom.

Ongoing Care

Grasses are the ultimate low-maintenance plant. Most will do very well with no supplemental feeding or watering, and they rarely get sick. But to keep them looking their best they may need the gardener's hand several times a year.

Watering and feeding

Most perennial grasses are drought-tolerant once established, but annual grasses, lacking extensive root systems, always appreciate water, and so do perennials in their first year of life. Water annuals as you would any flowers in the annual garden, about an inch a week. If rainfall is generous, they may need no supplemental watering. Water newly transplanted perennials every other day or every three days in well-drained garden soil. If your soil is light in texture or heavy in clay content, adjust your watering accordingly.

Additional water after the first year is not essential for perennials, but it will result in a lush plant that is taller and wider than usual. In drought conditions a grass may reach only half to two-thirds the size it does in a well-watered garden. But because grasses generally adapt to prevailing conditions, it's better not to start watering established plants in the spring if you don't plan to continue watering all season long — they'll suffer when the hose is withdrawn.

To provide supplemental water to established grasses, use soaker hoses or drip irrigation, or lay a garden hose directly at the plant's base. Overhead sprinklers are inefficient in delivering water directly to the roots and lose too much to evaporation. In humid climates they may also cause disease.

Grasses don't benefit from supplemental feeding, and they can in fact be hurt by it. Too much nitrogen can lead to either weak or rampant growth.

Staking

Some of the most beautiful grasses have a weak backbone that may not withstand uncommonly strong winds or other extremes of weather. Others will flop over from their own weight or size. To keep them standing erect, drive sturdy supports, such as thin metal pipes, into the earth and bind them with a cat's-cradle of strong twine or a loop of plastic-coated wire. Allow the plants some freedom of movement within the support so that they don't look like they're standing in a strait-jacket. The stakes can be camouflaged with green paint and hidden from view among the foliage.

Cutting back

Until recently, many gardeners trimmed back ornamental grasses as part of the fall cleanup. But a new appreciation of he beauty of weathering foliage, flowers, and seed heads has prolonged their presence through the winter, cut back earlier only if they become tattered or bare-looking. Most people cut back old foliage before new growth starts in spring, around the time early spring bulbs show their first shoots. Cool-season grasses can be cut back after they die out in the summer garden if you find their brown leaves unsightly. Often a stiff raking will be enough to remove old foliage. Grasses can also be cut back at other times of the year for other reasons. If, for example, a clump of miscanthus grass flops after a heavy rainstorm and doesn't recover in a few days, cut it back and t will shoot up again quickly.

While tolerance for untidiness dictates when and whether to cut grasses back, how much to cut can determine the future good health of your plant. As a general rule, don't cut grasses too short — in most cases that means leaving at least 4 inches of stubble. If you cut any shorter, you run the risk of clipping emerging new shoots that are hidden among the old stems, giving their tips a tattered look from which they won't recover. Leaving a few inches of old foliage also protects the crown and new shoots from weather extremes. Before you start slicing, pull apart the clump and check for emerging green shoots among the dead foliage. If you've missed on the timing, it won't hurt to cut a little higher than usual.

Effective grass cutters include hand shears or a trimmer with a metal blade (grass leaves tend to wrap around a string trimmer and jam it). Some gardeners take a chainsaw to particularly dense clumps. Keep a sharpening stone handy. The silica in grass rubs like sandpaper against the metal blades, dulling them like nothing else in the garden. Also look out for any metal supports you may have installed to help the clump stand up. They can be an unpleasant surprise when you're swinging a bladed trimmer.

Grass clippings from a spring shearing make a timely offering to garden birds for their nests. The long, dry leaves are favorites of sparrows and other songbirds. If you are handy, they can also be easily twisted into rustic wreaths, swags, or other long-lasting arrangements.

Division

Ornamental grasses can grow for decades without needing to be divided. But occasionally a clump will die out in the center and beg for renovation. Or you may want to collect a few starts from an existing plant to add elsewhere in the garden.

Running grasses are easy to divide. Using a spade or a trowel, dig up rooted pieces at any time during the growing season. Transfer them to new planting sites and water well.

Small clumping grasses aren't much more trouble. Divide them with a spade and a sharp knife in early spring when new growth begins. Just dig up the clump, wash enough soil from the roots to see what you're doing, then slice the plant into smaller pieces and transplant them.

Large clumping grasses require a lot more muscle and an arsenal of tools and gear because of their tremendous matted root systems. You'll need an axe or a wood saw instead of a shovel, gloves to protect your hands from sharp leaf blades, goggles to protect your eyes from leaf tips, and a strong back. First cut back the foliage by about a third. Dig around all sides of the plant with the shovel, slicing as deeply as you can under the roots. When the plant is loose, lever it onto its side; then either drag it to a work area or work in place. Spray off some soil from the root ball so the roots are easily visible, then hack the plant into sections with your axe or saw. Divide into still smaller pieces using a trowel or your hands. Replant the divisions quickly so the roots don't dry out.

If a plant has died out in the middle, you can try a "heart transplant" instead of digging the whole thing up and dividing it. Slice around the dead middle with a sharp spade, then pry it out with a crowbar. Add fresh soil in the center, and install a new plant of the same species.

Prairie burn

Nature maintains meadows and prairies with periodic fires, which clear accumulated debris, return nutrients in the debris to the soil, and eliminate woody and weedy invaders. Large-scale planted meadows or prairies can benefit from the same treatment every two to four years. Before contemplating a burn, do some planning. First find out if such fires are legal in your area and, if so, what precautions the fire department requires. A local wildflower or prairie restoration group or your county extension agent may be able to provide information on procedures and permits. Read a comprehensive publication on burning (try your extension service) to familiarize yourself with how it works, and then observe or help in a prairie burn before you attempt to set up your own.

Spring (late March to early May) is a good time for a burn. The warmed soil stimulates microbial activity, making nutrients available to plants, which respond with a burst of vigor. The moisture in the soil and in plants at that time of year means that a fire will move more slowly and therefore be easier to control than at other times of the year.

Start small, on half an acre or less, until you gain experience. Be sure to follow local regulations and notify neighbors and the fire department of your plans. You'll need at least three helpers to keep the fire under control. Specialized equipnent to put out fires and metal rakes to spread the flames are also a must. Don't try to get by with a garden hose; you'll need a water backpack/fire pump for control of the blaze. A grass fire may look tame compared to a forest fire, but it can quickly leap out of control.

Pests and Disease

Grasses are as disease- and pest-resistant as plants can be. Rust, an unsightly fungus, is their only disease, and it's not fatal. Aphids and grasshoppers may dine on the tender new growth. But grasses are quick to recover from these attacks. A bit more bothersome are pocket gophers. They can slice through grass roots with their sharp incisors and pull an entire plant down into their network of tunnels. Gardeners in coastal California and other areas of the West have learned to foil these grass thieves by lining the sides and bottom of planting holes with baskets made of chicken wire or hardware cloth. Rabbits, deer, and groundhogs may also occasionally dine on succulent grasses, but the rate of growth of new leaves soon outpaces any damaged foliage, which you can simply snip out.

Overcrowding on the one hand, and pampered conditions on the other, may increase the chances of rust in grasses. Though seldom a major problem, the fungal disease is unsightly, showing up as orange, powdery-looking patches on leaves and stems and causing them to turn yellow or brown and die. Rust can appear suddenly in the warm wet days and cool nights of spring, but vanish as rapidly when hot, dry weather comes. Poor air circulation or overhead watering can aggravate the problem. To prevent its possible occurrence, apply wettable sulphur in spring or during a humid summer. If signs of rust are already present, immediately clip off affected leaves and dispose of them in the trash. Also remove and replace mulch around infected plants. The disease overwinters in fallen leaves and other material.

Grasses in the Landscape

Grasses fit in everywhere in the home landscape. Here, 'Karl Foerster' feather reed grass stands out against a backdrop of trees and shrubs.

Growing 3–4 ft. tall, 'Yaku Jima' dwarf miscanthus is a perfect specimen grass for a small garden.

*Buffalo grass grows 4–6 in. high and makes a fine
naturalized lawn, though it goes dormant early.*

The fine-textured clumps of silver spear grass are equally at home in borders, naturalistic plantings, and near water.

A striking effect can be had with little effort or cost. A single tuft of blue oat grass adds enough contrasting color and form to set off the stand of 'Autumn Joy' sedum and the clump of feather reed grass behind.

The cool blue tones of some grasses brighten the yellows, pinks, or purples of perennials, giving these colors more mileage in the garden.

The feathery flowers of many grasses are more striking than their foliage. Long white plumes of feathertop stand out even more against the black-flowered 'Moudry' fountain grass.

This border devoted exclusively to grasses reveals their many shapes, sizes, and colors.

The last hurrah of summer, tall and mid-height grasses form a lush backdrop for the pincushion pods and woody stems of spent perennials. The grasses will continue to bleach silver and tan as fall and winter approach.

Botanical gardens and public landscaping sometimes offer imaginative grass plantings, like this border of grasses at Kew Gardens, in London, for ideas and specimens to incorporate into your own garden.

This "wild" border planted with grasses re-creates the sweep of nature's bounty.

'Gracillimus' maiden grass provides a background of fine green foliage for the airy panicles of variegated moor grass. Pairing grasses of substantial mass can have as great an impact as pairing grasses with shrubs.

Grass plumes left to weather in the winter landscape serve as a picturesque platform for snow.

Silver-leaved miscanthus contrasts with the low-growing
greenery in the foreground and bridges the transition to tall
shrubs and trees in the background.

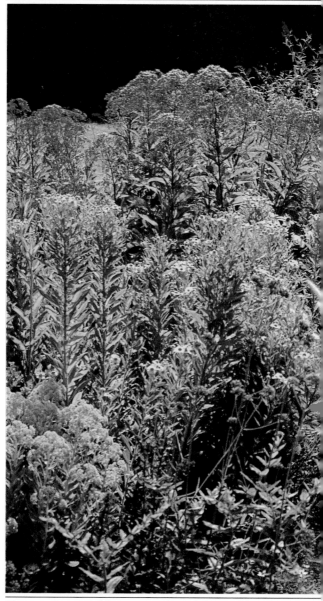

Treat grasses just like perennials in the mixed border, taking into account bloom time and height in relation to other plants.

The bright ribbons of Eulalia grass contrast in the late summer border with rusty red sedum.

Tall miscanthus grasses frame the modern lines of this raised patio and balcony and serve as attractive screens as well as points of interest.

The fine blades of 'Gracillimus' maiden grass are a perfect counterpoint to the flowers of the neighboring perennials.

Arching grasses grown in a pot can create the effect of a fountain. Even substantial grasses, like this crimson fountain grass, will readily adapt to life in a container.

Reflections in still water double the display of this evergreen miscanthus. Its reddish plumes will turn golden brown in fall.

Variegated miscanthus brightens the mostly green perennial border in late spring.

The metallic color of blue Lyme grass combines well with almost all perennials, but, like other running grasses, it has a tendency to overrun the perennial border.

The panicles of tufted hair grass reach up to 5 ft. high, but their delicacy and the low mounding habit of the foliage make this grass a good choice near the front of the border. Cool-season grasses like this one bloom in early summer, when other perennials are hitting their stride.

A bed of grasses in a farm garden takes on tones of silver and gold under a coating of frost. Many ornamental grasses keep color and form alive in the winter landscape.

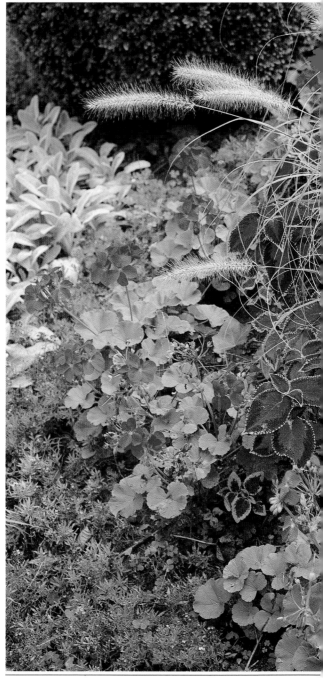

The shimmer of fountain grass above coleus and geraniums shows off these common annuals in a new way. You can grow tender perennial and annual grasses just as you would flowering annuals.

Ribbon grass is right at home in the annual border with snapdragons, salvia, heliopsis, and cosmos. Running grasses are usually not well enough behaved to be invited into the perennial border.

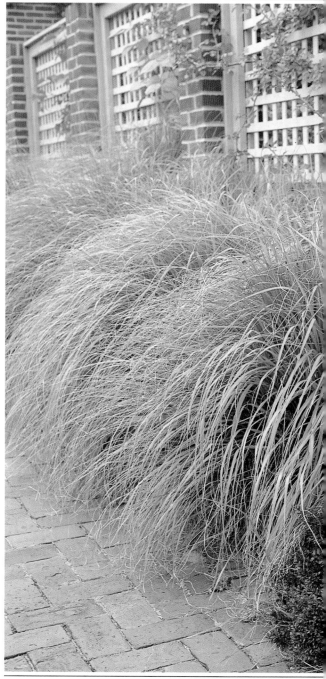

Lattice and brick create a handsome backdrop for the flowing fountain grass and the fiery 'Crimson Pygmy' barberry.

The ghostly shape of variegated miscanthus becomes the centerpiece of this wooded garden of hostas and foxgloves.

Many of the blue grasses, like this blue oat grass, are excellent plants to combine with spring bulbs — their fresh new growth complements the bulb flowers, and they soon grow to cover the yellowing bulb leaves.

Beds of ivy, tufted hair grass, and other grasslike ground covers light up a shady entry from late spring through summer.

Scattered among perennials and succulents on a rocky hillside, the sword-shaped clumps of grasslike New Zealand flax bring a wild look to the landscape.

The first in the wild to inhabit the most inhospitable sites, highly adaptable grasses are indispensable in a naturalistic setting.

Grasses are a natural around water. Fine-leaved sprays of contrasting colors add a fountainlike effect to this quiet lily pond.

Rock pools below this shaded gazebo are a natural setting for spearlike cattails and spidery umbrella plants grown in the water.

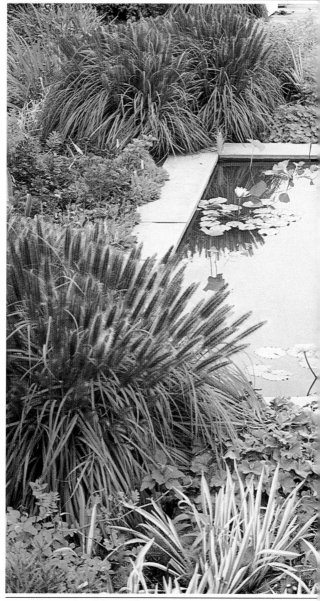

Mature stands of dwarf fountain grass lend a formal symmetry to the corners of this rectangular pool. The freely flowering grass plumes can be cut for fresh arrangements.

The earth tones of these clumps of fountain grass reflect the colors of the desert.

Mounding and tufted grasses are self-contained enough for rock gardens. Many of the drought-tolerant varieties used in dry gardens are cool-season western natives that go dormant in summer.

Gallery of Grasses

The photographs in this section will help you to put a "face" to the plants discussed in the essays and encyclopedia. They are organized alphabetically by genus and species. A short description accompanies each photo, along with the plant's botanical and common names, height, hardiness zone rating, and the page on which you'll find its encyclopedia entry.

A Word About Color

Color, more than many other visual attributes, is in the eye of the beholder. What one person describes as blue, another may call lavender, or even purple. Compounding these differences of opinion are the effects of light and shade, time of day, and nearby colors on what we actually see. Grasses exhibit a narrower range of colors than more flamboyantly flowering plants, but this in some ways complicates the problem, requiring us to distinguish among a myriad of greens, blue-greens, buffs, browns, and golds.

As you look at the photos on the following pages, remember that the camera, no less than the eye, captures color as it appears at a certain moment and season. Add to that the natural variation among plants and the difficulty of printing colors precisely, and you'll see why it doesn't pay to count on your plant having exactly the color you see in the photograph.

| **Achnatherum calamagrostis** | *Silver spear grass Height 18–36 in. Clumping grass with fluffy flower heads that persist through winter Zone 6–9* | *Good for borders, naturalistic plantings, along water or ponds p. 182* |

| **Acorus calamus** 'Variegatus' | *Variegated sweet flag Height: 2–3 ft. Bold foliage, stripes can be creamy white to yellow Zones 5–10* | *Use for accent in moist to wet soils or in water p. 184* |

orus gramineus
gon'

Golden variegated
Japanese sweet flag
Height: 10 in.
Use as accent or
mass planting in
garden or by pond
Zones 6–9

Sun or part sun;
good container
plant.
p. 184

ropyron
agellanicum

ue Magellan
ass
eight: 12–18 in.
milar to blue
me grass without
vasiveness
nes 5–8

ot suited for hot,
mid conditions
186

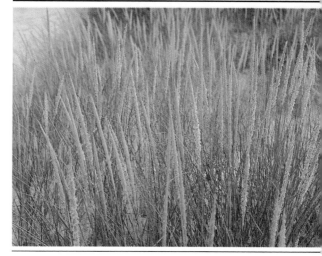

Ammophila breviligulata

*American beach grass
Height: 2–3 ft.
Evergreen ground cover for sandy soils
Zones 4–7*

*Use for naturalist plantings on coastal sites
p. 187*

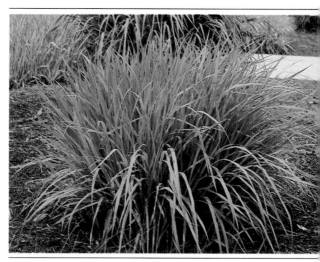

Andropogon gerardii

*Big bluestem
Height: 4–8 ft.
Foliage and flowering stalks striking in summer and fall
Zones 4–9*

*Use as accent in large border or massed
p. 188*

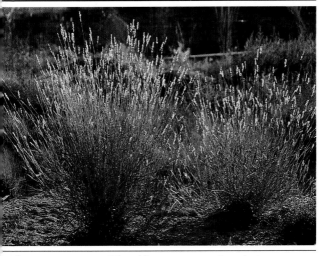

Andropogon
saccharoides

Silver bluestem
Height: 12–18 in.
Southwest native;
seed heads
attractive when
backlit
Zones 5–9

Lovely in a
meadow planting
p. 189

Aristida purpurea

Purple three-awn
Height: 12–30 in.
Flowering stems
turn from purple to
bleached blond
Zones 6–9

Good for
naturalized
plantings in dry
conditions
p. 190

***Arrhenatherum elatius* var. *bulbosum* 'Variegatum'**	*Variegated bulbous oat grass* *Height: 8–24 in.* *Narrow leaves have thin green stripe; flowers not decorative* *Zones 4–9*	*Good for front to middle of mixed border* *p. 191*

Arundinaria viridistriata	*Running bamboo* *Height: 30 in.* *New leaves gold with green stripes* *Zone 4*	*Use as ground cover where spread can be contained* *p. 192*

| *Arundo donax* | Giant reed
Height: 9–25 ft.
Fall bloom in mild
climates
Zones 6–10 | Good accent plant
with water features
p. 193 |

Arundo donax
'Variegata'

Striped giant reed
Height: 5–12 ft.
Leaf color turns
greener during
season
Zones 8–10

Evergreen in mild
climates
p. 194

Bambusa oldhamii

Giant timber bamboo
Height: 50–55 ft.
Clumping bamboo with stems up to 4 in. thick
Zone 8

Use like trees to mark entry or for screening
p. 194

Bouteloua curtipendula

Sideoats grama
Height: 2–3 ft.
Clump-forming; flowering stalks in early summer
Zones 4–9

Meadow or prairie plantings
p. 195

outeloua gracilis

lue grama grass
eight 8–24 in.
ed heads
corative for long
eriod
ones 3–10

est in mass
antings
196

riza media

erennial quaking
ass
eight: 2–3 ft.
reen spring
owers turn tan
ith age
ones 4–8

ood front- or
id-border plant
197

Buchloe
dactyloides

Buffalo grass
Height: 4–6 in.
Flowers
insignificant; greens
up late, browns
early
Zones 3–9

Good for
naturalized lawn
p. 198

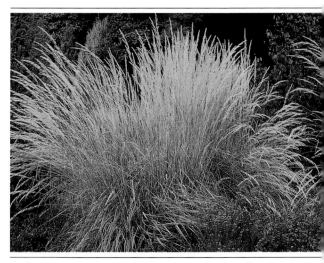

Calamagrostis
acutiflora
'Karl Foerster'

'Karl Foerster'
feather reed grass
Height: 5–6 ft.
Tall flower stalks
showy summer
through fall
Zones 5–9

Full or part sun in
wet or dry soil
p. 199

| *Calamagrostis acutiflora* 'Stricta' | Feather reed grass Height: 5–7 ft. Blooms May to June; can be evergreen in warm climates Zones 5–9 | Use in border, as specimen, or with mixed grasses p. 199 |

| *Calamagrostis nutkaensis* | Pacific reed grass Height: 2–4 ft. Early to midspring flowers Zones 8–9 | Summer-drought-tolerant ground cover p. 200 |

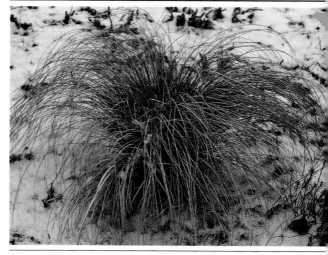

Carex buchananii	Leatherleaf sedge Height: 2 ft. Shiny reddish brown tufts in summer; rarely flowers Zone 6	Use in border with blues and whites p. 201

Carex comans	New Zealand hair sedge Height: 12–24 in. Fine-textured rolled leaves are green, brown, or whitish green Zones 7–9	Good along water p. 201

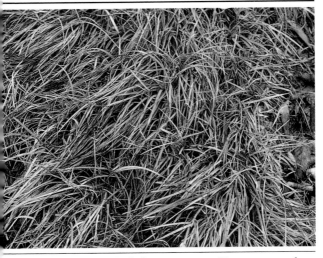

Carex nigra

Black-flowering
sedge
Height: 6–9 in.
Unusual black
flower spikes rise
just above foliage
in spring
Zones 4–8

Use as a ground
cover or pond
edging
p. 203

Carex petriei

Dwarf brown sedge
Height: 4–6 in.
Ever-brown ground
cover; flowers add
a curly effect
among leaf tendrils
Zones 7–9

Needs moist but
well-drained soil
p. 203

Carex plantaginea

Plantain-leaved sedge
Height: 12–24 in.
Versatile ground cover; foliage stays green well into winter
Zones 4–9

Use as accent among woodland plants
p. 204

Carex siderosticha 'Variegata'

Creeping variegated broad-leaved sedge
Height: 12–24 in.
Grows in a sweeping colony of bold foliage
Zones 5 or 6–9

Use as a spot accent or ground cover
p. 204

| Chasmanthium latifolium | Northern sea oats Height: 3–5 ft. Clump-forming perennial grass with broad leaves and dangling seed heads Zone 4 | Use as border accent or ground cover on slopes or open woodland p. 206 |

Coix lachryma-jobi

Job's tears
Height: 3–6 ft.
Ungainly plant grown for unusual teardrop seeds
Zones 9–10

Perennial in mild climates; plant as annual from seed in cold areas
p. 207

*Cortaderia
selloana*

*Pampas grass
Height: 8 ft.
Feathery plumes
showy from late
summer through
midwinter
Zone 7*

*Nearly evergreen in
warm climates; use
as specimen,
barrier hedge, or
wind screen
p. 207*

*Cortaderia
selloana* 'Pumila'

*Dwarf pampas
grass
Height: 4–6 ft.
Flower plumes rise
to 5 ft. in late
summer
Zones 8–10*

*Good with colorful
shrubs
p. 209*

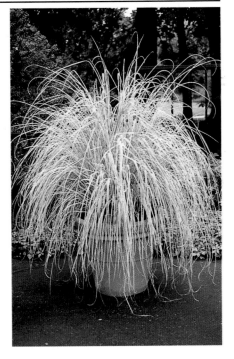

Cortaderia
selloana
'Silver Comet'

'Silver Comet'
pampas grass
*Height: 6–8 ft.
White-striped
leaves distinguish
this cultivar
Zones 7–10*

*Fine specimen
p. 209*

Cymbopogon
citratus

*Lemongrass
Height: 2–6 ft.
Fragrant leaves
used in tea and
cooking
Zones 9–10*

*Tender perennial
thrives in
containers in cold-
winter areas
p. 210*

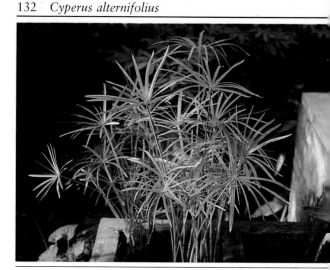

| *Cyperus alternifolius* | Umbrella plant Height: 18–36 in. Forms elegant clumps of umbrella-like leaves Zones 9–10 | A natural near water or with bog plants p. 212 |

Cyperus papyrus

Egyptian papyrus
Height: 6–15 ft.
Long bracts form
arching sprays on
stout stems
Zones 9–10

Water garden or
patio showpiece
p. 213

Cyperus profiler

Dwarf papyrus
Height: 12–36 in.
Stiff bracts make
this a livelier
version of the
refined umbrella
plant
Zones 9–10

Good scale for
small pool or
aquarium
p. 213

Dasylirion
texanum

Sotol
Height: 2–3 ft.
Mounding plant
with slender flower
stalks up to 15 ft.
tall
Zones 8–10

Useful for desert
gardens; can be
grown in a
container
p. 214

| *Deschampsia caespitosa* | *Tufted hair grass Height: 2–3 ft. Evergreen or semievergreen; blooms late spring through summer Zones 4–9* | *Excellent for mass plantings p. 215* |

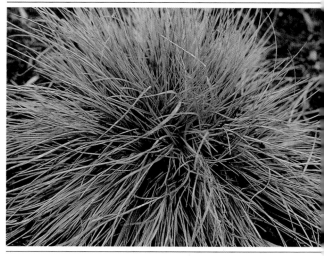

| *Deschampsia caespitosa* 'Bronzeschleier' | *'Bronze Veil' tufted hair grass Height: 2–3 ft. Drooping bloom almost hides foliage Zones 4–9* | *Use cut flowers in bouquets p. 215–216* |

| eschampsia
uespitosa
'Goldgehange' | 'Gold Pendant'
tufted hair grass
Height: 2–3 ft.
Single plant
commands
attention
Zones 4–9 | Grow along water
or in woodland
garden
p. 216 |

| lymus arenarius
'Glaucus' | Blue Lyme grass
Height: 1–2 ft.
Invasive mound-
forming grass with
sharp-tipped blue
leaves
Zones 4–10 | Use in border with
sunken barriers;
controls erosion in
all soils
p. 218 |

Elymus condensatus 'Canyon Prince'

'Canyon Prince' wild rye
Height: 18–24 in.
Less invasive cultivar; flower spikes rise to 6 ft.
Zones 7–9

Use in mixed border or foliage garden
p. 218

Elymus tritichoides

Creeping wild rye
Height: 2–4 ft.
Fast-spreading native of American West
Zones 7–10

Use as ground cover or in mass plantings
p. 219

Equisetum hyemale

Scouring rush
Height: 18–48 in.
Upright perennial
with striking bare
stems; native to wet
places but grows
anywhere
Zones 5–10

Dark green stems
keep their color
all year
p. 219

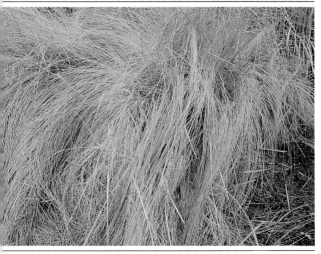

Eragrostis curvula   Weeping love grass   Plant on slopes, in
Height: 12–24 in.   border
Mounding habit;   p. 221
drought-tolerant;
evergreen in mild
climates
Zones 7–10

Erianthus ravennae

Ravenna grass
Height: 9–12 ft.
A hardy
pampaslike grass;
silky plumes last
through winter
Zones 6–10

Large plant for
screens or tall
border
p. 223

Eriophorum latifolium

Cotton grass
Height: 8–18 in.
Forms colonies of
thin spiky leaves;
woolly flowers in
spring
Zones 4–8

A light-hearted bog
plant for cool
gardens
p. 224

Festuca amethystina	Sheep's fescue Height: 8–12 in. Cool-season evergreen; gray-blue flowers in late spring Zones 4–8	Fine edging or border plant, or as short-lived ground cover p. 225

Festuca gautieri	Bearskin fescue Height: 4 in. Alpine native; drought-tolerant perennial Zones 4–6	Plant in shady rock gardens or in pots; needs good drainage p. 226

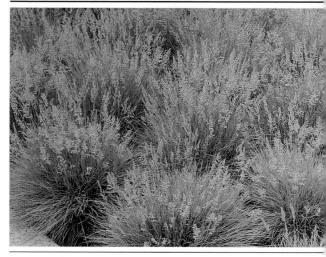

| *Festuca glauca* 'Blau Silber' | 'Blue-Silver' fescue Height: 8 in. Clumping evergreen; stands up to summer heat Zones 4–9 | Edging, rock garden, container p. 227 |

| *Festuca glauca* 'Elijah's Blue' | 'Elijah's Blue' fescue Height: 8 in. One of the palest cultivars; medium texture Zones 4–9 | Striking with deep purples, reds, and other strong-colored flowers p. 228 |

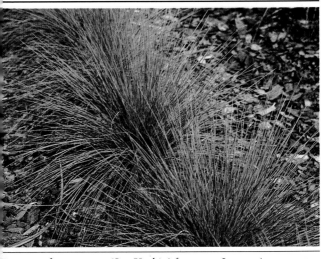

| *Festuca glauca* 'Sea Urchin' | 'Sea Urchin' fescue *Height: 8 in. Springy green clump; extra-fine texture Zones 4–9* | *Interesting accent, good edging or ground cover* p. 228 |

| *Festuca muelleri* | *Mueller's fescue Height: 6–8 in. Cool-season perennial; fine green foliage Zones 5–9* | *Needs light shade in hot climates* p. 228 |

Glyceria maxima
'Variegata'

Manna grass
Height: 2–6 ft.
Reedlike perennial
with erect-arching
habit; spreads fast
Zones 5–10

Aquatic grass for
large ponds
p. 229

Hakonechloa
macra

Hakonechloa
Height: 12–30 in.
Japanese native
grass; green leaves
turn orange-bronze
in autumn
Zones 4–10

Finest shade
specimen or ground
cover; spreads
slowly
p. 230

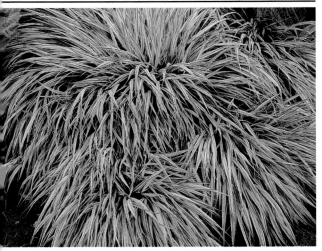

Hakonechloa macra 'Aureola'

Golden hakonechloa
Height: 12–24 in.
Cascading foliage; fall color intensifies to pink
Zones 4–10

Combines with greens in shade garden
p. 230

Helictotrichon sempervirens

Blue oat grass
Height: 12–36 in.
Large clump-forming perennial grass with spiky leaves; blue intensifies in dry soil
Zones 4–9

Use as foundation plant, ground cover
p. 231

| *Helictotrichon sempervirens* 'Saphirsprundel' | 'Sapphire Fountain' blue oat grass Height: 24 in. Dense arching tuft with clear blue-gray leaves Zones 4–9 | Superb in perennia border as single accent or massed p. 232 |

| *Hordeum jubatum* | Foxtail barley Height: 12–30 in. Short-lived perennial grass; distinctive flowers in early summer Zones 4–10 | Grow as annual in masses or for cut flowers p. 232 |

| *Hystrix patula* | Bottlebrush grass
Height: 24–48 in.
Perennial
woodland grass;
flowers persist
through fall
Zones 4–9 | Good shade-garden
grass
p. 233 |

| *Imperata*
cylindrica
'Red Baron' | Japanese blood
grass
Height: 12–18 in.
Perennial creeper;
bright red foliage;
seldom flowers
Zones 6–9 | Fine accent plant;
use as edging for
lawn or border, or
massed on slopes
p. 234 |

Juncus effusus

*Soft rush
Height: 18–48 in.
Expands gradually
by creeping roots
Zones 4–9*

*Adds a natural
look to water
gardens but is
adaptable to dry
soil
p. 235*

**Juncus effusus
'Spiralis'**

*Corkscrew rush
Height: 12–24 in.
Semievergreen
oddity of coiling
stems; flowers not
showy
Zones 4–9*

*Thrives in moist
locations
p. 235*

uncus patens

*California gray
rush
Height: 18–30 in.
Slender, erect form;
foliage bluish green
year-round
Zones 8–9*

*Very adaptable
p. 236*

Koeleria argentea *Silver hair grass
Height: 12–18 in.
Cool-season
perennial;
handsome two-
toned leaves
Zones 6–9* *Use as ground
cover in sunny,
well-drained sites
p. 236*

Koeleria glauca

*Large blue hair grass
Height: 6–24 in.
Dainty evergreen tufts; best in lean, sandy soil
Zones 6–9*

*Use for edging or massing
p. 237*

Koeleria macrantha

*Crested hair grass
Height: 12–18 in.
Perennial; erect tufted habit; variable gray-green color
Zones 2–9*

*Use in naturalistic meadow
p. 237*

gurus ovatus	Hare's tail Height: 12–24 in. Soft green tufts go unnoticed once blooms appear in summer All zones	Grow from seed in annual bed; use in cut-flower arrangements p. 238

zula nivea nowbird'	'Snow Bird' snowy wood rush Height: 8–12 in. Forms small clumps of velvety gray leaves Zones 4–9	Fine perennial for shade or woodland garden p. 238

Melica ciliata

Hairy melic grass,
silky spike melic
Height: 8–12 in.
Perennial cool-
season; flowers in
late spring or early
summer
Zones 5–8

For casual border
or cut flowers
p. 240

**Miscanthus
floridulus**

Giant Chinese
silver grass
Height: 8–12 ft.
Pyramidal flower
plumes in fall
Zones 5–9

Use as specimen,
hedge, or
windbreak; needs
no staking
p. 242

| *Miscanthus sacchariflorus* | Silver banner grass
Height: 4–8 ft.
Foliage turns tan;
flowers attractive
for months;
invasive
Zones 5–9 | Good for wet
meadow or pond
edging
p. 243 |

Miscanthus sinensis 'Cabaret'

'Cabaret' miscanthus
Height: 6–8 ft.
Pink blooms in early fall
Zones 7–10

Use as specimen, border backdrop, screen
p. 245

**Miscanthus
sinensis
'Cosmopolitan'**

'Cosmopolitan'
*miscanthus
Height: 6–8 ft.
Abundant coppery
red plumes in fall;
needs no staking
Zones 7–10*

*Large specimen or
accent
p. 245*

**Miscanthus
sinensis
'Flamingo'**

'Flamingo'
*miscanthus
Height: 5–6 ft.
Lush foliage; long
feathery plumes
Zones 6–9*

*Use as specimen or
along water
p. 245*

**Miscanthus
sinensis
'Gracillimus'**

*Maiden grass
Height: 5–8 ft.
Copper-red tassels
in midautumn
Zones 5–9*

*Grow as specimen;
may need support
p. 246*

**Miscanthus
sinensis 'Graziella'**

*'Graziella'
miscanthus
Height: 5–6 ft.
Fine leaf texture;
summer-blooming
Zones 5–9*

*Smaller miscanthus
for mixed border
p. 246*

**Miscanthus
sinensis 'Kascade'**

*'Cascade'
miscanthus
Height: 5–7 ft.
Blooms early and
for long periods
Zones 5–8*

*Good in mixed
border; specimen
grouping; near
water
p. 246*

**Miscanthus
sinensis
'Kleine Fontaine'**

*'Little Fountain'
miscanthus
Height: 3–4 ft.
Compact grass;
extended bloom
time
Zones 6–9*

*Excellent in front
of taller grasses or
in the mid-ground
of the border
p. 246*

| *Miscanthus sinensis* 'Morning Light' | *'Morning Light' miscanthus* Height: 4–5 ft. Deep pink-bronze flowers in early to midfall Zones 5–9 | *Plant by itself or in groups, with woody or evergreen shrubs* p. 246 |

| *Miscanthus sinensis* 'Purpurascens' | *Flame grass* Height: 3–4 ft. Compact; fall foliage color holds into winter Zones 4–8 | *Plant alongside shrubs with bright fall foliage* p. 247 |

**Miscanthus
sinensis
'Silberfeder'**

*'Silver Feather'
miscanthus
Height: 6–9 ft.
Cascading foliage
and flowers;
summer-blooming
Zones 5–9*

*Plant with
evergreen shrubs,
near a pool or pon*
p. 247

Miscanthus sinensis 'Undine'	*'Undine' miscanthus Height: 4 ft. Slender, compact grass; warm fall color Zones 5–9*	*Good size for mixed border* p. 248

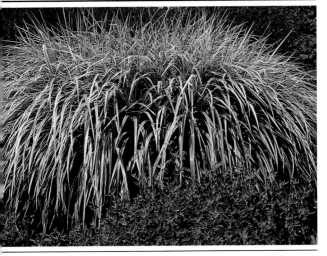

**Miscanthus
sinensis
'Variegatus'**

Variegated
miscanthus
Height: 6–9 ft.
Abundant pink
flowers 1–2 ft.
above foliage in
early fall
Zones 6–9

Tolerates shade
p. 248

**Miscanthus
sinensis 'Zebrinus'**

Zebra grass
Height: 6–8 ft.
Wide-arching
clumps may need
support
Zones 6–9

Popular at water's
edge
p. 248

| *Miscanthus transmorrisonensis* | Evergreen miscanthus Height: 3–4 ft. Spring-blooming in mild climates, early to midsummer in cool climates Zones 7–10 | Fine specimen p. 249 |

Molinia caerulea 'Heidebraut'

'Heather Bride' moor grass
Height: 2–3 ft.
Compact green tufts with abundant, tall flower stalks
Zones 5–8

Bloom adds vertical line to garden
p. 250

| Molinia caerulea p. litorialis | Tall moor grass
Height: 2–3 ft.
Flowers rise 6–9 ft.
above low, dense
tufts in summer
Zones 5–8 | Use in border or
naturalistic garden
p. 250 |

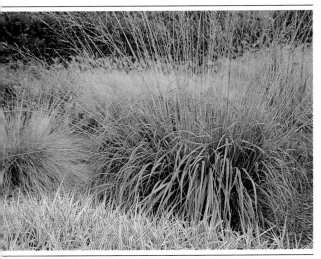

| Molinia caerulea p. litorialis kyracer' | 'Skyracer' tall moor
grass
Height: 2–3 ft.
One of the tallest
in bloom; straight
flower stems rise
7–8 ft.
Zones 5–8 | Adds architectural
accent
p. 250 |

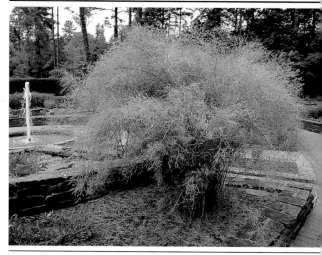

Muhlenbergia dumosa

*Bamboo muhly
Height: 3–9 ft.
Cool-season
perennial; arching
foliage resembles
fine bamboo
Zones 8–10*

*Heat- and drough
tolerant
p. 251*

Muhlenbergia pubescens

*Soft blue Mexican
muhly
Height: 8–12 in.
Low-mounding
perennial; downy
evergreen foliage;
gray-blue flowers
Zones 9–10*

*Plant in groups or
singly
p. 252*

| *Muhlenbergia rigens* | Deer grass
Height: 2–4 ft.
Western cool-season native;
green foliage holds color through summer
Zones 7–9 | Use in naturalistic dry garden, or as hillside ground cover
p. 253 |

| *Oryzopsis hymenoides* | Indian rice grass
Height: 12–30 in.
Cool-season tufted grass; delicate panicles open in spring
Zones 7–10 | Good in a xeriscape with perennials and silver-foliaged plants
p. 254 |

Panicum virgatum | Switch grass
Height: 3–7 ft.
Good fall color;
flowers held high
above leaves in
summer
Zones 5–9 | Tolerates wet and
dry sites
p. 256

Panicum virgatum
'Cloud Nine' | 'Cloud Nine'
switch grass
Height: 4–6 ft.
Medium-tall
clumping perennial;
flowers persist into
winter
Zones 5–9 | Plant in a meadow
groupings
p. 256

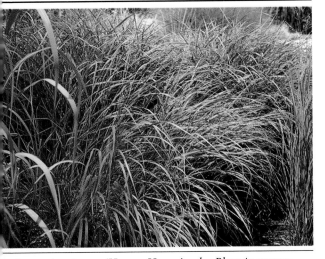

***anicum virgatum* 'Haense Herms'**	'Haense Herms' red switch grass Height: 3–4 ft. Flowers and foliage suffused with red in early autumn Zones 5–9	Plant in masses, borders p. 256

***anicum virgatum* 'Heavy Metal'**	'Heavy Metal' switch grass Height: 3–5 ft. Columnar form; unusual blue-gray foliage turns yellow in fall Zones 4–9	Outstanding mixed-border plant; maintains form in the winter garden p. 257

| *Panicum virgatum* 'Rotstrahlbusch' | 'Red Rays' red switch grass Height: 3–4 ft. Excellent red fall foliage Zones 5–9 | Plant in the mixed border; in grouping or drifts p. 257 |

| *Panicum virgatum* 'Squaw' | 'Squaw' switch grass Height: 3–4 ft. Loose habit; purple-red leaves by late summer Zones 4–9 | Partner with warm or cool-season grasses or shrubs with good fall colo p. 257 |

Pennisetum alopecuroides 'Cassian'

'Cassian' fountain grass
Height: 12–24 in.
Dwarf cultivar; soft flower spikes reach 3 ft. high
Zones 4–9

Perfect for the front of the border
p. 258

Pennisetum alopecuroides 'Moudry'

Black-flowered fountain grass
Height: 2–3 ft.
Unusual black flowers; variable bloomer; invasive in mild climates
Zones 7–9

Shade-tolerant
p. 259

| *Pennisetum macrostachyum* 'Burgundy Giant' | 'Burgundy Giant' fountain grass Height: 4–5 ft. Flowers in midsummer; grow as annual in cold climates Zones 9–10 | Combine with other grasses, shrubs, and perennials in a protected site p. 259 |

| *Pennisetum orientale* | Oriental fountain grass Height: 1–2 ft. Early blooming; grow as annual in cold climates Zones 7–9 | Beautiful near water, as a specimen or in a group p. 260 |

*Pennisetum
setaceum
'Rubrum'*

Crimson fountain
grass
Height: 2–3 ft.
Tender cultivar;
mounding fine-
textured burgundy
foliage
Zones 9–10

Grow as annual in
cold climates
p. 261

*Pennisetum
villosum*

Feathertop
Height: 24–30 in.
Tender perennial;
fluffy foxtails all
summer; can be a
pest in Midwest
and South
Zones 8–9

Good for coastal
gardens
p. 261

***Phalaris arundinacea* 'Feesey'**	*'Feesey' ribbon grass* *Height: 2–3 ft.* *Fine leaves blush pink in spring; showy white flowers in summer* *Zones 4–9*	*Invasive; grow as ground cover or provide barriers* *p. 262*

***Phalaris arundinacea* 'Picta'**	*Ribbon grass* *Height: 2–4 ft.* *Warm-season running grass; invasive in all but very dry gardens* *Zones 4–9*	*Grow as ground cover or as aquatic in shallow water* *p. 262*

ormium tenax

*ew Zealand flax
eight: 8–9 ft.
rge grasslike
int with 5-in.-
de spear-shaped
ves
ones 8–10*

*ll stalks of
ddish flowers in
mmer
263*

**yllostachys
reosulcata**

*Yellow groove
bamboo
Height: 15–20 ft.
Highly invasive
plant will form
groves
Zones 6–10*

*Handsome screen
when contained
p. 264*

Phyllostachys nigra

Black bamboo
Height: 10–25 ft.
Striking culms ideal
for Japanese garden
Zones 7–10

Invasive; grow in
containers
p. 264

Rhynchelytrum repens

Natal grass
Height: 1–4 ft.
Short-lived
clumping perennial;
long bloom time
Zones 9–10

Rampant self-sower
in warm climates
p. 266

sa veitchii

Silver-edge bamboo
Height: 2–3 ft.
Low-spreading,
broad-leaved
bamboo; holds
color all winter
Zones 7–10

Ground cover for
shade or traditional
Japanese garden
p. 268

*hizachyrium
oparium*

*ttle bluestem
eight: 2–3 ft.
airie native;
ender green
liage in summer
ones 3–9*

aturalistic
antings, large-
ale ground cover,
 in the mixed
order
269

| *Semiarundinaria murielae* | *Running bamboo*
Height: 10–15 ft.
Tall, dense, slow-spreading bamboo;
clump creates
weeping-willow
effect
Zones 7–10 | *Trouble-free; use*
screen
p. 272 |

| *Sesleria autumnalis* | *Autumn moor grass*
Height: 18 in.
Evergreen, shade-tolerant
Zones 5–9 | *Plant in sweeps*
p. 273 |

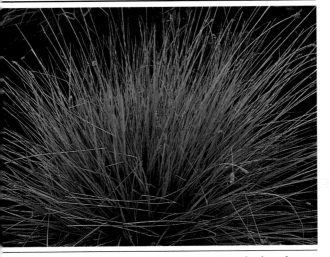

Sesleria
eufleriana

Green moor grass
Height: 12–18 in.
Young leaves
powdered with
white
Zones 5–9

Tough plant for
rock gardens
p. 273

Sorghastrum
nutans

Indian grass
Height: 3–8 ft
Perennial tallgrass
prairie native; good
fall and winter
color
Zones 4–9

Use as accent, in
border, or as screen
p. 274

Sorghastrum ***nutans*** **'Sioux Blue'**	*'Sioux Blue' Indian* *grass* *Height: 3–5 ft.* *Silvery blue cultivar* *with very erect* *habit* *Zones 4–9*	*Use as single* *specimen or plant* *as mass* *p. 275*

Spartina pectinata	*Prairie cord grass* *Height: 4–6 ft.* *Perennial running* *grass with arching* *sharp-edged leaves* *Zones 4–9*	*Thrives along* *water; more* *restrained in dry* *soil* *p. 275*

**podiopogon
biricus**

*ost grass
eight: 2–3 ft.
ow-spreading;
amboolike foliage
rns colorful in
ll; pretty flowers
late summer
ones 5–9*

*lant as specimen
in masses in sun
shade
, 276*

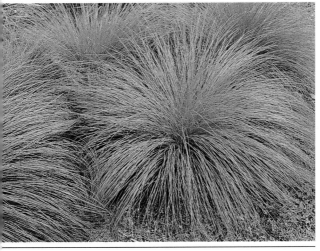

**porobolus
eterolepsis**

*Prairie dropseed
Height: 18–30 in.
Mounding
perennial grass;
fine leaves turn
orange and gold in
fall
Zones 4–8*

*Easy-care plant
anywhere in the
garden
p. 277*

Stipa gigantea

Giant feather grass
Height: 2–3 ft.
Cool-season
perennial flowers
late spring to early
summer
Zones 7–9

Specimen,
naturalized
planting
p. 279

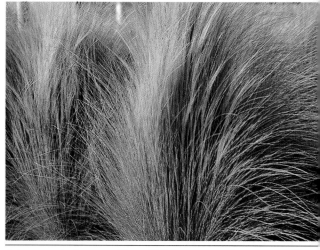

Stipa tenuissima 'Pony Tails'	'Pony Tails' Mexican feather grass Height: 12–18 in. Silky flowers from late spring through fall Zones 7–10	Aggressive self-sower; plant in a naturalized meadow p. 280

**Tripsicum
dactyloides**

*Gama grass
Height: 6–10 ft.
Striking male and
female flowers
Zones 4–9*

*Thrives near water,
in shade
p. 281*

Typha latifolia

*Cattail
Height: 3–5 ft.
Perennial rushlike
plant for wet sites;
velvety brown
pokers persist
through fall
Zones 4–9*

*Colonizes rapidly
around and in
shallow water
p. 282*

Uniola paniculata *Sea oats*
Height: 3–8 ft.
Perennial coastal
native; spreads
slowly by creeping
rhizomes
Zones 7–10

Needs sandy soil;
sensitive to foot
traffic
p. 283

Vetiveria
zizanioides

Vetiver
Height: 4–10 ft.
Perennial warm-
season grass;
evergreen in frost-
free climates
Zones 9–10

Native to wet
places but tolerates
drought
p. 284

ucca filamentosa

*ear grass
Height: 2–3 ft.
Evergreen perennial
with swordlike
leaves and very
showy flowers in
une
Zones 5–10*

*Grow in average to
ry soils; requires
ttle care
. 284*

Zea mays

*Ornamental corn
Height: 3–15 ft.
Various cultivars
offer colorful leaves
and decorative ears
Zones 4–9*

*Grow as a hedge or
background
planting
p. 286*

Encyclopedia
of Grasses

e plants described in this section are organized alphabeti-
lly by genus. A short description of the genus is followed
 individual entries for featured species and cultivars. These
tries pack a lot of information into a small space. We hope
ey will be easy to follow. Here are a few comments to help
u make the best use of them.

ames

ant taxonomists are continually reclassifying plants and re-
ming the groupings to which the plants are assigned, mak-
g any book outdated almost before it appears. This is par-
ularly true of grasses. We have tried to use names and
assifications current at the time of writing, but have in-
uded synonyms by which many nurseries (and taxonomists)
ay still identify the plant.

haracteristics

he beginning of each entry provides certain basic informa-
n about the plant for quick reference, including its com-
on names, its hardiness zone rating, and its height and
read. In addition, we have used abbreviations to indicate
hether the plant is an annual (A), perennial (P), or peren-
al grown as an annual (PGA). Clump-forming grasses (Cl)
e distinguished from running grasses (R); and warm-season
asses (W) from cold-season grasses (C), a distinction drawn
ly for plants in the grass family (Gramineae). Some grasses
e neither clumping nor running, and their habits are dis-
ssed in the text.

Achnatherum

Ak-nath′er-um
Gramineae. Grass family

Cool-season perennial grasses with loose, arching foliag
and soft spears of flowers. As with many grasses, the bota
ical name of this genus and its species is debated by taxon
mists. Some consider the grasses of this Eurasian genus a pa
of the genus *Stipa*, which includes related needle grasses ar
spear grasses of North America, South America, Europ
Asia, and Australia.

■ *calamagrostis* *p. 116*
(Stipa calamagrostis)
Silver spear grass, reed grass, silver spike grass
Zones 6–9. P/Cl/C
Height: 18–36 in. Spread: 24 in. or more

A mid-height clumping grass of fine texture with beautif
fluffy flower heads. The narrow plumes of flowers are he
about 6 in. above the leaves on arching stems that follow tl
graceful sweep of the foliage. The flower heads have a silk
purplish sheen when newly emerged in June and change 1
glistening silvery white and finally to deep tan. Flowers pe
sist through winter. Leaves turn amber in fall, then lighten 1
tan in winter. In mild-winter climates, the foliage may reta
some green through most of the year.

The graceful, abundant flowers at a moderate height mak
silver spike grass an asset in borders, groups, or naturalist
plantings, where it can hold its own even with aggressiv
perennials such as pink evening primrose *(Oenothera sp
ciosa)*. It is also attractive along streams or ponds. For a
ethereal combination, plant lady's-mantle around the feet c
this grass and wait for a heavy dew. The soft plumes of gra
flowers collect droplets of dew like a fine silver net, while tl
wide, pleated lady's-mantle leaves beneath are spangled wit
larger droplets.

How to Grow

Full or part sun; water regularly for best growth. Thrives 1
a wide range of soils, from clay to loam. Spreads moderate
in loose, moist soil; heavy or dry soils keep it in a clum
Originally from the cool mountains of Europe, this grass la1
guishes in hot, dry climates. Cut back in early spring. Divic
in spring or throughout growing season. Flowers are good i
fresh or dried bouquets and swags.

corus

ı-kor´us

aceae. Arum family
Perennial plants of marshes and wetlands, which sprout
ns of irislike leaves from fleshy rhizomes. The plants thrive
wet soil, but they adapt to life in average garden soil, and
me also flourish in containers. The genus includes only two
ecies, from Europe, Asia, and the Far East. The roots of
orus calamus, or sweet flag, were brought to England and
er to America as part of the early pharmacopeia, and today
is plant can be found growing thickly along moats and
kes around old British castles and in wet places from Nova
otia to Minnesota, south to Kansas and Louisiana.

calamus

veet flag
nes 4–10. P/R
eight: 24–36 in. Spread: 18–24 in. or more
This slender-leaved plant looks like an iris or a big grass,
ıt it's really a relative of the classic calla lily and the famil-
r wildflower, Jack-in-the-pulpit, which you can see by the
ıb-shaped flowering spadix, typical of the arums. Sweet flag
beautiful along the water's edge, where its tall, erect 1-in.-
ide leaves rustle and move in the wind. Wild stock can
ach 6 ft. tall, but most nursery plants top out at 3 ft. or
ss. The odd but sweetly fragrant flowers stick out from the
ıf stems at 45° angles. The linear form of the plants is a
od foil for the enormous rounded leaves of rodgersia or
ınnera. The slim blades also look good when combined with
e arrowhead leaves of blue-flowered pickerelweed.
The thick, long, branching roots are pungently aromatic;
itish aristocrats once powdered their wigs with scented
wder made from them. The roots have also been used as
ıvoring, in candy, or distilled in oil for perfume, as well as
medicinal remedy. (The FDA disapproved medicinal use
ter tests showed it to be carcinogenic.) The leaves are nicely
agrant and in the days of chamber pots and infrequent
thing were used as a "strewing herb," spread on floors to
eate a pleasant scent.

ow to Grow

ıll sun to light shade. Boggy or moist soil high in organic
atter. Will also tolerate standing water of several inches'
pth, and will thrive in garden soil of average moistness.
st at water's edge, where it spreads at a moderate pace. Di-
de in spring or fall, digging up a piece of rhizome and re-
anting.

■ *calamus* 'Variegatus' *p. 116*
Variegated sweet flag
Zones 5–10. P/R
Height: 24–36 in. Spread: 12 in. or more

A striking, boldly striped version of sweet flag, this cul
var looks yellow at a distance. Its creamy white to yello
stripes make it an attention-getter in the garden; use it as a
accent among green-foliaged plants, or with blue or whi
Siberian or Japanese irises or glowing yellow monkey flow
(*Mimulus* spp.). Leaves are about 1 in. wide.

How to Grow
Like *A. calamus*. Branching, creeping rhizomes spread mo
slowly than the species.

■ *gramineus*
Japanese sweet flag
Zones 7–9. P/R
Height: 6–12 in. Spread: 8 in. or more

A downscaled version of sweet flag, with narrow leav
like thick, lush grass. The species reaches 12 in. tall, b
dwarf cultivars as short as 5 in. are also available. The glos
$1/2$-in.-wide leaves are wonderfully fragrant, which makes th
plant a perfect choice for edging walkways or as a grour
cover, where foot traffic will release the fragrance. You ca
even use it in place of lawn grass in small areas. Its sprea
ing roots also find a home among rocks, such as in an info
mal garden or between stepping-stones or along a pool ed
ing. The soil stays cool and moist beneath the rocks, and th
swords of leaves are a good contrast in line and texture.

How to Grow
Sun or part sun. Moist or well-watered soil; perfect for th
edges of ponds or other water features, where it will thri
in wet soil. Also makes a good container plant, if frequent
watered. Leaf tips die back when water is scarce. Gradual
spreads into a seamless turf. Propagate by division in sprir
or fall. Spider mites may web the undersides of the lush f
liage, causing the upper sides to become mottled and sickl
wash off the pests with a blast of water from the garden ho
or cut back the leaves to ground level and let them regrow

■ *gramineus* 'Ogon' *p. 117*
Golden variegated Japanese sweet flag
Zones 6–9. P/R
Height: 10 in. Spread: 12 in. or more

Beautiful golden yellow, fine-textured foliage produced
abundance has a casual attitude, arching in various directio

e a tousled head of hair. Its color will light up a partly
ady spot or draw attention to a pond or pool. Plant at a
nd in a path to catch the eye and draw the feet onward. If
u plant it where late afternoon sun can shine through the
iage, the plant will almost glow with warm color. Try
lden variegated sweet flag in a mass planting. The leaves
e only $\frac{1}{8}$–$\frac{1}{4}$ in. wide, which keeps even a large planting
m becoming an overpowering presence.

ow to Grow

n or part sun. Flourishes in moist soil, but will also grow
ll in garden soil of average moisture. A good container
ant. Well suited for planting near water.

gramineus 'Variegatus'

riegated Japanese sweet flag

nes 7–9. P/R

eight: 6–12 in. Spread: 6 in. or more

This small but eye-catching cultivar grows in tufts of
eamy white-striped fine-leaved foliage. Plant as individual
cents or in a mass. (They spread slowly, so plant close to-
ther.) Try the cool green-white of variegated sweet flag with
stand of high-voltage red cardinal flower, or use this
asslike plant in the foreground of a group of waterside
ants of similar upright habit but coarser texture and greater
ture.

ow to Grow

ght shade. Flourishes in moist soil, but will also grow in
rden soil of average moisture. Excellent along water.

Agropyron

Ag-roe-py´run

Gramineae. Grass family

Cool-season perennial grasses of clumping habit, with tu[...] of fine-textured foliage. Most often used for hay, pasture, [...] lawn grass, but also includes outstanding ornamentals, [...] well as one of the worst garden pests, quack grass *(Agrop[...] ron repens).* The genus is closely related to wheat *(Triticu[...] aestivum),* and some botanists believe that wheat may ha[...] developed as a hybrid with this genus. (The name *Agropyr[...]* is from the Greek *agrios,* wild, and *puros,* wheat.) About [...] species, native to and widely distributed throughout t[...] Northern and Southern Hemispheres.

■ *magellanicum   p. 117*
(Elymus magellanicus)
Blue Magellan grass
Zones 5–8. P/Cl/C
Height: 12–18 in. Spread: 12–18 in.

Dense, spiky tufts are an ethereal gray-blue, the color [...] the best blue spruces. The $1/4$–$1/2$-in.-wide leaves are similar [...] appearance to blue Lyme grass *(Elymus arenarius* 'Glaucus[...] but the clumping plant lacks the rampant invasive tendenci[...] of that species. Flowers look like heads of wheat and are a[...] pealing in arrangements. The seed heads ripen to tan, but t[...] grass may stay evergreen, especially in mild-winter climate[...] Be careful working around Magellan grass; its leaves can [...] sharp and prickly.

The small tufts are easy to incorporate with floweri[...] perennials. The gray-blue color is beautiful with pink flowe[...] such as dianthus, and it makes yellow and white flowe[...] stand out with extra dash. Hot pink and magenta are cool[...] by the blue grass, which works well when planted in grou[...] as a transition between colors. Also a good companion f[...] red-leaved barberries.

The cultivar 'Longwood' is shorter than the species (to [...] in.) with equally striking foliage that appears light blue [...] gray-green depending on your vantage point.

How to Grow

Full sun. Moist, well-drained soil. Thrives in coastal cond[...] tions, even when exposed to salt spray. Not suited for h[...] humid conditions; not drought-tolerant. Cut back once a ye[...] to encourage new, brightly colored growth.

mmophila

ı-moh´fill-uh

ramineae. Grass family

Erect, perennial grasses of sandy shores, with long, tough, arp-pointed leaves and far-reaching rhizomatous roots. Inudes only four species.

breviligulata p. 118

merican beach grass

ones 4–7. P/R/W

eight: 24–36 in. Spread: 36 in. or more

Long, thin, gray-green leaves rise from tough rhizomatous ots that spread widely in sandy soil. Plants grow in loose lonies, throwing up new shoots far from the mother plant. af blades are tipped by dangerously sharp points that are threat to the eyes of dogs, children, and others. Blooms in te July or August, with long, narrow, soft-textured spikes sembling golden tan pipe cleaners. Flowers persist until eir stems break from coastal winds.

In its native range, the East Coast and the Great Lakes, merican beach grass is useful in home landscapes for coving a steep bank because it spreads fast and needs no mainnance. It also makes a good low-maintenance ground cover r a naturalistic yard, where it can be combined beautifully ith native lupines in shades of blue, white, and yellow. Sparws nest in the hillocky clumps.

The introduced European species, *Ammophila arenaria* uropean beach grass), was once a favorite for dune stabiation but has proved so invasive on the West Coast that it listed by the California Native Plant Society as one of the ost problematic weeds. It threatens coastal sand dune sysms by outcompeting native dune plants and interfering with e natural dynamics of dune systems. On the Atlantic Coast, greatly alters beach profiles and subsequently changes the npact and effect of storms on the coastline.

ow to Grow

ıll sun or part sun. Sand or sandy soil. If planting in pure nd, set out new divisions at least 10 in. deep, where the nd feels moist. The buried roots will soon take hold and nd up new shoots. Propagate by division in spring or fall.

ndropogon

ı-dro-po´gun

ramineae. Grass family

Perennial, warm-season grasses of varying habit, some tall

and clumping, others short and creeping. Includes one of the main grasses of the American tallgrass prairie. About 20 species, native to temperate and tropical regions throughout the world.

■ *gerardii* p. 118
Big bluestem, turkeyfoot, turkey claw, beardgrass, bluejoint
Zones 4–9. P/Cl/W
Height: 48–96 in. Spread: 24 in. or more

One of the dominant grasses of the American tallgrass prairie that once covered millions of acres, big bluestem is being discovered by gardeners for its ornamental effects and undemanding attitude. It is a willowy grass of great height, but most of its foliage stays in an erect, slightly arching clump of gently curling leaves that usually reaches about 2–3 ft. tall. Its soft, 1/4-in.-wide foliage is lead-gray to bluish green when it emerges in spring; plants vary in their blueness when young, as well as in their retention of the color as they mature, with most turning green. At bloom time in late summer and early autumn, the flowering stems rise to the height of a person or taller. The distinctive 3-angled flowers look like turkey foot jutting off the top of the skinny, gangly stems. The plant is beautiful in fall, when it takes on warm tan, bronze, and crimson hues. The colors are softened in winter to warm russeted tan with glints of red and bronze; the foliage persists through winter although the seed heads soon shatter.

This clumping plant is a beauty in prairie plantings or in groups of grasses. It's also a treasure in the mixed border. Despite its height, you can place it in the midground of the border as well as the back because its tall flowering stems are no

ick with leaves. The plant has an almost see-through qual-
, like the flowering *Verbena bonariensis;* in fact, the two
ake a great combination of purple and russet. The clustered
ikes of perennial Maximilian sunflower and the drooping
llow petals of prairie coneflower are good partners, as are
ll asters in shades of blue and pink.

'Roundtree' has an erect, upright habit of growth and is
mewhat smaller in stature than the species, reaching 6 ft.
ll under average conditions. It comes into bloom earlier, a
od attribute for gardeners with shorter growing seasons.
he Blues' is another erect-growing cultivar with excellent
ue-gray color and vertical line. Both are beautiful with pink
tilbe.

ow to Grow

ll sun. Average garden soil, including clay. Young plants
ay seem slow to grow, but they are busy establishing ex-
nsive root systems that will be able to withstand consider-
ile drought after three years or longer in the garden. Big
uestem tolerates high summer heat and thrives in humidity
 well as dryness. In fertile soil, with abundant rain, the
ants can reach 10 ft. tall; under less favorable conditions,
e plants are more frugal in their growth and may top out
 4–6 ft. Cut back in early spring. Self-sows readily in ideal
nditions. Propagate by division or seed in spring. Use 15
ounds of seed per acre when planting a large area in grass
one or 10 pounds per acre if including flowers and other
ants.

saccharoides p. 119
Bothriochla saccharoides)
lver bluestem, silver beardgrass
ones 5–9. P/Cl/W
leight: 12–18 in. Spread: 12 in. or more

Native to the American Southwest, silver bluestem forms
ick tufts of fine leaf blades that sprout delightful little puffs
f silvery white seed heads at the tops of slim, erect, 2–3-ft.
owering stems. In fall, the grass turns rich colors of purple
 pumpkin orange that mellow a bit during the dormant sea-
n but still hold enough color to be a welcome sight in the
inter. Once used for hay, silver bluestem is a beautiful ad-
ition to the garden, especially when naturalized in a meadow
r on a slope where the sun can backlight the fluffy hairs of
e eye-catching seed heads.

ow to Grow

ull sun. Average garden soil. Cut back in early spring. Prop-
gate by seed or division.

Anthoxanthum
an-tho-zan´thum
Gramineae. Grass family

Annual or perennial cool-season grasses with fairly sho
tufts of soft, fine-textured leaves that have a wonderful ar
matic fragrance. About six species native to Eurasia a
North Africa. The species below is naturalized in the easte
United States and along the Pacific Coast.

■ *odoratum*
Sweet vernal grass
Zones 5–10. P/Cl/C
Height: 12–24 in. Spread: 6 in. or more

This cool-season clumping perennial grass smells like fres
cut clover when its leaves are crushed or crumpled. Th
dense, spiky-looking but soft tufts stay about 6 in. tall, wi
12–18-in. flowering stems emerging to spray out over th
plant. The grass is evergreen, but the slender spikes of flowe
bloom in spring and soon dry to golden brown. You can cl
them off or cut back the grass for a neater look.

Sweet vernal grass is not particularly showy, but it is nic
when planted in grassy footpaths, spilling onto pathways,
in a lawn area, where its scent can be enjoyed as the leav
are bruised by foot traffic. Kids and adults alike enjoy pullir
a sweet-tasting flowering stem to nibble. You can cut leav
and twist them into small, fragrant knots or wreaths for ir
doors; they hold their scent for a long time after cutting.

How to Grow
Full sun or part sun. Average garden soil. Plant in light shac
in areas with scorching summer sun. May self-sow. Propaga
by seed or division.

Aristida
uh-ris´tih-duh
Gramineae. Grass family

Perennial clumping grasses of the American shortgra
prairie. Formerly ignored by horticulturists, the genus includ
several decorative species that are valuable in naturalisti
landscaping in hot, dry areas such as the desert Southwest.

■ *purpurea* *p. 119*
Purple three-awn
Zones 6–9. P/Cl/C
Height: 12–30 in. Spread: 12 in.

This heat-tolerant perennial grass forms dense but airy

oking tufts of rolled, $\frac{1}{32}$–$\frac{1}{16}$-in.-wide leaves that often curl
d twist. The "three awns" of the seed heads have very long,
ky hairs that catch the light like spiderweb threads in the
n. The feathery, delicate flowering stems grow 18–30 in.
ll, but are often loose and lax. They have a purple sheen
at matures to platinum blond above the golden tufts of fo-
ge.

Plant this grass where it can naturalize, which it will do by
eding itself. Keep it away from traffic, and avoid planting
if you have long-haired pets — the bristled seed heads catch
clothing and fur and can become painful irritants as the
edlelike awns coil tightly to "plant" the seed in your pants
g or other inappropriate place.

ow to Grow

ll sun. Average garden soil. Tolerates drought and heat.
ropagate by seed or division in spring. Purple three-awn is
native grass of the American shortgrass prairie, which once
overed the west-central United States. Grasses from this area
e well adapted to the dry conditions found in the rain
adow of the Rockies; their roots are short and wide-spread-
g, and the plants typically grow in spaced clumps (bunch-
asses), so that each benefits from as much moisture as pos-
ble.

rrhenatherum

-ren-ath´ur-um
ramineae. Grass family

Perennial grasses of varying habit, including a useful pas-
re grass for humid regions and an old-fashioned favorite or-
amental grass. Includes six species, all native to the Mediter-
nean region.

elatius var. *bulbosum* 'Variegatum' *p. 120*

ariegated bulbous oat grass, variegated tuberous oat grass
ones 4–9. P/R/C
eight: 8–24 in. Spread: 8–12 in.

The ghostly color and short to medium height of this
erennial cool-season clumping grass make it a prize in the
erennial border. Its narrow leaf blades are about $\frac{1}{8}$–$\frac{1}{4}$ in.
ide and look spiky but are soft to the touch. From a dis-
nce, the grass glows silvery white; only at close range do
ou notice the thin green stripe along the center of each leaf.
he narrow panicles of flowers, which look like bristly wild
ats, emerge in late spring to early summer, but they're not
specially decorative, and the grass is not at its best by then.

The luminous tuft of leaves looks great with perennials and bulbs that flower in early to late spring, when oat grass is at its peak. It's also fun to play with foliage effects, such as combining its narrow, spiky form and color with the broader, silver-spangled leaves of lungwort and waterleaf. It's beautiful with blue catmint, especially the taller cultivar 'Six Hill Giant' and with hardy geraniums of all colors. When the grass begins to sprawl and flag in summer, even before blooming, many gardeners cut it back hard and let other plants, such as baby's-breath or perovskia, take its place. If you give it generous water after cutting back, the foliage may sprout anew. When you cut back the clump, note the unusual bulbous nodes from which the grass sprouts, jointed like short vertical strings of children's pop-it beads.

How to Grow
Full sun to part sun. Moist, well-drained soil. Plant in light shade in areas with hot summers. May be infected by the rust virus; immediately cut off and remove any orange-blotched or yellowing foliage. Divide any time of the growing season, giving new starts generous water until they're established.

Arundinaria
A-run-di-nayr´ee-a
Gramineae. Grass family
    Hardy bamboos with spreading rhizomes and leafy upright stems. Flowering is rare; when it occurs, all members of a species flower simultaneously over a large area. About 30 species, native to the Old and New Worlds.

■ *viridistriata* p. 120
(now *Pleioblastus viridistriatus*)
Running bamboo, golden bamboo
Zone 4. P/R
Height: 30 in. Spread: indefinite
    The new leaves of this dwarf spreading bamboo are vibrant gold with bright green stripes. It is invasive but less so than other small running bamboos. Useful as a ground cover to control erosion on steep banks or as a tough, low-maintenance cover for areas surrounded by concrete sidewalks or drives. Use it to brighten a shady corner or woodland edge, and try interplanting it with gold or purple crocuses, yellow narcissus, and red or purple tulips. Can be grown in a container on a deck or patio. *A. variegata*, 13 ft. in height, is similar but has white-striped leaves; it runs aggressively and must be confined.

ow to Grow

olerates shade, but sun makes the leaves a brighter yellow.
rdinary soil and watering. Hardier than formerly acknowl-
lged; tops freeze back, but runners survive. Buy one to start
ith; you can soon divide it if you want more. Use hand
uners or a string trimmer to mow off old stems in spring.

rundo

ı-run´doe
ramineae. Grass family

Tall, perennial, reedlike grasses with broad leaf blades and
umed flowers. About six species, native to tropical and sub-
opical areas of the Old World.

donax *p. 121*

iant reed, giant cane, carrizo
ones 6–10. P/R/W
eight: 9–25 ft. Spread: 36 in. or more

Tallest of the ornamental grasses, this species can reach 20
. or higher in ideal conditions of moisture and year-round
armth. Garden-grown plants in cold-winter areas usually
ɔp out at about 10–12 ft. Giant reed looks like a huge bam-
ɔo, with leaves that can reach 3 in. wide and 24 in. long.
arge soft flower panicles bloom in fall in mild climates; in
old areas, the plants may not bloom. Giant cane turns beige
ith the onset of cold weather, and the leaves rattle coarsely
ı the wind. The thick, jointed stems have been used for thou-
ınds of years for homebuilding, lattices, and animal fences
. some countries. Split stems are used for reeds in woodwind
ıstruments (sections of stem were also once used for organ
ipes in Europe).

In the garden, giant reed is best used as an accent near
·ater, where its gangly height looks most at home. The large
umps expand by rhizomatous roots, which grow fast in
ild-winter climates and make giant reed a poor choice for
ardeners in such areas. The plant is much less invasive in
reas with cold winters, where it can make a fast-growing
edge or windbreak.

ow to Grow

un. Average garden soil. Moist soil and frequent watering
ncourages aggressive root growth. Plant in spring. Cut back
ld foliage in early spring; use woody old stems for plant
ıpports in perennial or vegetable garden. Propagate by divi-
on or take cuttings of rhizomes in early spring.

■ *donax* 'Variegata' *p. 121*
Striped giant reed
Zones 8–10. P/R/W
Height: 5–12 ft. Spread: 36 in. or more

This statuesque plant has broad leaves striped with white, cream, or yellow, which give it a golden appearance, especially at the top of the plant. The color turns greener as the leaves age during the season. Under average garden conditions, striped giant reed stays about 5–7 ft. tall. Like the plain green species, plants are taller and more robust in mild-winter areas or when given plenty of moisture. In cold-winter areas, this grass makes a good tall accent in a mixed planting with miscanthus and other large-size grasses. Striped giant reed is evergreen in mild climates, but freezes to beige in cold weather.

How to Grow
Like *Arundo donax.*

Bambusa

Bam-boo´sa. Bamboo
Gramineae. Grass family

Clump-forming bamboos, some with large woody culms. About 100 species, native to tropical and warm climates.

■ *oldhamii* *p. 122*
Giant timber bamboo
Zone 8. P/Cl
Height: 50–55 ft. Spread: 20 ft.

Truly a giant, it makes a huge green fountain for tropical or Oriental effects. The stems are green, turning yellow, up to 4 in. thick, and make good poles for fencing or other garden structures. The thin, bright green leaves are up to 12 in. long. Use single plants or pairs to mark an impressive entry. Plant with bananas, elephant's-ear, or gingers for a tropical look. This bamboo is a clumper. Another giant timber bamboo, *Phyllostachys bambusoides,* is a runner and will in time form open groves to 45 ft. tall, with 6-in. stems. It is hardier (Zone 7) than *B. oldhamii.*

How to Grow
Full sun. Ordinary soil and watering okay, but grows larger with fertile soil and ample water. One plant is usually enough. For a really big screen to block undesirable views, plant 10–15 ft. apart. To divide old plants, use pick, axe, and saw in spring. The fallen leaves of all bamboos may be considered

tter, or you could think of them as an attractive, weed-sup-
ressive mulch.

Bouteloua

oot-uh-loo´uh

Gramineae. Grass family

These fine-bladed perennial and annual warm-season
grasses are mainstays of natural grasslands in North and
South America and are still used as pasture and forage
grasses. Named after the Bouteloua brothers of Spain, who
were among the first to cultivate a native grass for use in gardens, they make a good addition to naturalistic garden plantings because of their interesting flowering spikes. About 50
species, native to the Americas from the central United States
to Argentina. All are commonly known as grama grasses.

curtipendula p. 122
sideoats grama, sideoats gramma
Zones 4–9. P/Cl/W
Height: 24–36 in. Spread: 18 in.

This clumping perennial grass has wonderfully decorative
flowers that dangle like a line of little bells from one side of
the graceful flowering stems. They're as pretty in a vase as
they are in the garden. Plants grow in a dense clump of fine
leaves, usually reaching 1–2 ft. tall. The abundant, gently
arching flowering spikes emerge in early summer, sprouting a
foot or more above the foliage. Native sparrows and other
birds feast on the seeds. The stems persist through winter,
mellowing to golden yellow after first taking on a purple hue
with frost.

This is a beautiful plant for a meadow or prairie garden. Its soft tufts of narrow, $1/8$–$1/4$-in.-wide leaves combine easily with the simple blooms of native wildflowers such as California poppies or mallows. In winter, a mass planting of the standing clumps provides shelter for birds and small mammals. It can also be used as a lawn grass.

How to Grow

Sun. Very tolerant of soil, thriving equally well in poor, sandy soils; heavy clay; or rich, loose loam. Drought-tolerant. Plant seed or divisions in spring. Propagate by seed or division. May self-sow, but unwanted seedlings are easily smothered by mulch. Mow or clip each year to about half its height to remove old seed stems and clean out dead thatch. As a lawn, mow to about 2–4 in.; it will spread densely. Tolerant of foot traffic.

■ *gracilis* p. 123
Blue grama grass, blue gramma grass
Zones 3–10. P/Cl/W
Height: 8–24 in. Spread: 6–12 in.

Formerly propagated for use as a pasture grass, blue grama is gaining acceptance as an ornamental thanks to its diminutive size, which makes it easy to use in gardens, and its interesting flower heads, which are tightly bunched into thick little brushes that jut out from the stems at 45° angles. The grass blooms in summer, and seed heads remain decorative for a long time. Like sideoats grama, this grama grass turns purplish with cold weather, then gradually changes to a warm tan for winter. Blue grama also makes a hardy, drought-tolerant lawn grass in arid regions.

How to Grow

Sun. Any soil, except for wet soils or heavy clay. Another tough grama grass, this species will withstand extremes of heat, drought, and cold. It self-sows generously, but since it looks best in mass plantings, that trait is usually not a problem. Plant seed or divisions in spring. Mow large plantings or cut back individual plants in early spring to remove old foliage. Propagate by seed or division. If plants develop "fairy ring" (center of clump dying out), dig out center, add fresh soil, and insert a few new divisions.

Briza

i´zuh

Gramineae. Grass family

A widespread genus of annual and perennial grasses with showy panicles of dangling, trembling seed heads that are widely used in dried arrangements. The botanical name is from the Greek *brizein,* to nod. About 20 species, native to Eurasia, the Mediterranean, and other temperate regions, and widely naturalized in North America.

media *p. 123*

Perennial quaking grass
Zones 4–8. P/Cl/W
Height: 24–36 in. Spread: 12–18 in.

This perennial cool-season grass bears erect panicles of small round seed heads that look almost like dainty white baby's-breath flowers from a distance. The plants form small clumps of soft, $1/4$–$1/2$-in.-wide foliage, usually about 12–18 in. tall. Flowers rise well above the plant, where their charming form can be easily seen. The wiry stems that hold each seed head to the main flowering stem look thin and fragile, but they're surprisingly strong, and the panicles persist for several weeks after flowering in spring. Bright green at first, they soften to warm tan, with the seeds shivering and rattling at the slightest breath of wind.

This is a fine grass for the perennial border because its dangling of dainty flowers bloom in mid- to late spring, accenting their neighbors. Because of the see-through quality of the flowers, you can plant it in the foreground or middle without obscuring other plants. It's also good in masses or meadow plantings.

Annual quaking grass *(B. maxima)* is a smaller plant, its seed heads large, flattened, pointed ovals that hang like pennants from very thin, wiry stems. This easy-to-grow plant is appealing in the garden (sow seed where plants are to grow) and its seed heads are long-lasting in dried bouquets. Let them dry to tan on the plant before cutting, or they'll retain a green color.

How to Grow

Full sun. Average soil. Easy to grow. Cut back and water well after blooms shatter to encourage fresh growth. Plant divisions in spring, or in fall in mild-winter climates. Propagate by division.

Buchloe

boo-clo´ee
Gramineae. Grass family
   This genus includes only a single species, the perennial stoloniferous buffalo grass native to the Great Plains of North America.

■ *dactyloides* *p. 124*
Buffalo grass, buffalo reed grass
Zones 3–9. P/R/W
Height: 4–6 in. Spread: 6 in. or more
   Buffalo grass is perfect for those who hate mowing lawns; it never gets any taller than a few inches, and it spreads to form a fine-textured, gray-green turf. Flowers are short and not a distraction. Unfortunately, the curling leaf blades turn dull beige with cold weather and stay that way until late spring. Many prefer it naturalized rather than mown. The stoloniferous roots are superb at holding soil, making this plant an excellent choice for ground cover on a slope. Lark sparrows, horned larks, and other birds appreciate the seeds.

How to Grow
Full sun. Any soil. Tolerates drought but not wet soil. Plant seeds thickly in pots (they're slow to sprout), or set out divisions in spring. Plugs are available for planting large areas; plant these 4-in. sections about 24 in. apart. This is a tough plant that actually does better in poor soils than in fertile ones. It is slow to spread — a new lawn of buffalo grass may look patchy for its first couple of years. Water very deeply, to 1 ft., every month for the first growing season. Once the grass is established, the runners expand quickly to knit a thick turf. Avoid overwatering once established; abundant moisture increases the height of the plants. Keep buffalo grass away from perennial borders, where its stolons may invade.

Calamagrostis

kal-uh-muh-grahs´tis
Gramineae. Grass family
   Annual or perennial grasses that form large erect clumps with tall, fairly narrow plumes of flowers. Some are important forage grasses, especially in the West. The botanical name refers to their resemblance to reeds: from the Greek *kalamos,* a reed, and *agrostis,* a kind of grass. About 25 species, native to the temperate zones.

acutiflora **'Karl Foerster'** *p. 124*
. × *acutiflora* 'Karl Foerster')
arl Foerster' feather reed grass
ones 5–9. P/Cl/C
eight: 5–6 ft. Spread: 24 in.

A strongly vertical plant that makes an exclamation point
the garden, it provides good contrast to low-mounded
rennials or shrubs. Makes a clump of very slender, wiry
aves 3 ft. long, with much taller flower stalks spiking up
rough the center of the clump. The flowers appear in June;
e seed heads, slim as pipe cleaners, look pretty all summer
d fall as they turn from gold to silver. Leave it untouched
the end of the season; this grass is strong enough to
eather the vagaries of winter. 'Sierra', another fine upright
ltivar, turns a rich, warm golden brown in late summer.

ow to Grow
ll or part sun. Ordinary to poor soil. Tolerates either wet
dry conditions. Divide and plant in spring or late summer.
ut back in early spring.

acutiflora **'Stricta'** *p. 125*
Calamagrostis acutiflora* var. *stricta*)
ather reed grass
ones 5–9. P/Cl/C
eight: 5–7 ft. Spread: 24 in.

An outstanding grass for the border, for specimen use, or
r a mixed grass grouping, this beautiful plant forms dense,
ft.-tall clumps of $1/4$–$1/2$-in.-wide leaves, with flowering
ems rising stiff and straight from the middle of the plants
create a dense vertical column. The flowering stems rise
-4 ft. above the foliage and are topped by airy golden
umes, wider and more open than those of *C. a.* 'Karl Foer-
er'. 'Stricta' blooms in May to June, like a cool-season
ass, but it is often evergreen or nearly so in mild-winter cli-
ates, where it may refuse to bloom regularly. In cold areas,
e foliage ripens to tawny golden orange and persists
roughout winter, making a beautiful accent, especially in
ow.

The strong vertical line and stature of feather reed grass
ake it a good plant for the back of the border, where it can
fronted by yarrows, marguerites, shastas and other daisies,
d other perennials of loose or mounded habit.

ow to Grow
ll sun. Moist soil. Thrives in clay soils. Plant divisions in
ring, or in spring or fall in mild-winter climates. Cut back
early spring. Propagate by division.

■ *brachytricha*
(*C. arundinacea* var. *brachytricha*)
Korean feather reed grass, fall-blooming feather reed grass
Zones 4–9. P/Cl/W
Height: 3–4 ft. Spread: 24–36 in.

At the end of the gardening season, the soft white plume of Korean feather reed grass spill over boltonias, aster *Sedum spectabile,* and the last of the garden flowers. Th clumping perennial grass is a warm-season grower that form 18–24-in.-tall mounds of foliage in spring and summer. wealth of feathery flowers arise at the end of summer for grand finale. The smoky purple blooms mature to pale beig while the foliage takes on the color of ripe wheat. The flowe are much fatter and fluffier than the usual narrow spikes the other feather reed grasses, and the whole plant has a mo casual, arching attitude.

How to Grow

Full sun to part sun and light shade. Moist soil. Plant in lig shade in hot-summer regions. Water generously during d weather. Plant divisions in spring. Cut back in early sprin Propagate by division in early spring or fall.

■ *nutkaensis* p. 125
Pacific reed grass
Zones 8–9. P/Cl/C
Height: 2–4 ft. Spread: 12–18 in.

West Coast hikers may encounter this native species coastal meadows along the Pacific, where the shaggy clum may cover a large area. A cool-season perennial, it thrusts pointed spears of $1/2$–$3/4$-in.-wide leaves in a dense tuft. Pa icles of early to mid-spring-blooming flowers stand 1–2 above the foliage and soon turn from purplish to warm ta

This is not a grass for the garden, but it does make a goc ground cover or low-maintenance planting in coastal and dr summer areas. It is extremely tolerant of summer drought a thrives in the "serpentine" soils of the West Coast, where na ural minerals in the green rock known as serpentine discou age the growth of many plants. This is the dominant nati bunchgrass under Monterey pines in Pebble Beach and on tl Monterey Peninsula in California. Pacific reed grass als flourishes in the windy, salt-spray extremes of coastal lan scapes, where it can be used as a luxuriant mass on stee banks or combined with shrubs such as Santa Barbara cea othus (*Ceanothus impressus*).

How to Grow

Full sun to partial shade. Thrives in a wide range of soil

om deep, moist soil to clay to rock, and including serpen-
ne. Plant divisions any time from early spring to fall. Cut
ack in late fall to make way for fresh winter growth. It's eas-
st to propagate by division, although the plants may occa-
onally self-sow. Best established by planting nursery-grown
ugs, which are about $1\frac{1}{2}$ in. across and 4–6 in. deep.

Carex

re´ex
yperaceae. Sedge family

A huge genus of grasslike perennials, most forming tufts
clumps of slender leaves. All sedges bear clusters of sepa-
te male and female flowers on solid, 3-sided stalks. More
an 1,000 species, found worldwide but especially in cool,
et climates.

buchananii *p. 126*
eatherleaf sedge
one 6. P/Cl
eight: 2 ft. Spread: 1 ft.

Making an airy tuft of shiny cinnamon-colored foliage, the
ne delicate leaves arch gracefully and curl at the tips.
eatherleaf sedge offers relief from the green that dominates
l gardens, but it also complements blue, white, or reddish
own plants. Combine it with silver-leaved thyme and yel-
w primroses for winter and spring. It rarely flowers.

ow to Grow

art sun or shade. Ordinary or better soil. Space 1 ft. apart
r mass plantings. Divide in spring. Cut foliage back in late
ll or early spring. In cold climates, grow one in a container
nd bring it indoors to a sunny window for the winter.

comans *p. 126*
(*Carex comans* 'Stricta'; *C. albula*; *C. vilmorinii*)
ew Zealand hair sedge
ones 7–9. P/Cl
eight: 12–24 in. or larger. Spread: 12–18 in.

This common weed of New Zealand pastures is one of the
ost beautiful ornamental grasses for the garden. Its excep-
onally fine-textured leaves spill into dense tussocks that look
ke a mop of shining, light green hair. Natural variations in
olor and habit frequently occur, but all forms of the plant
e attractive, whether the leaves are green, brownish, or
hitish green. A close look will show that the leaves are
olled almost cylindrically. The plant is often nonflowering.

This sedge can tolerate cold as low as –10°F; if you're a Zo:
6 gardener, it's worth chancing it.

New Zealand hair sedge thrives in very moist soil and
perfect along water, where its flowing mane of foliage can
reflected for double the glory. Try it with the contrasting ve
tical spears of statuesque Japanese iris, or let it be the star
the moist garden, rising from a carpet of blue forget-me-no
or golden moneywort. It is also a solo performer in a lar
clay pot, where its fine leaves can drape over the side.

The cultivar 'Bronze' looks like a miniature version of t
species (growing to 12 in.), but it stays brown year-roun
and it isn't quite as flowing. Once you get over the initi
"dead-plant" look, you'll find the unusual color combin
well with pink flowers or with purple-leaved shrubs such
smokebush. Interesting to grow not only for its own meri
but as a practical joke on garden visitors.

How to Grow
Full sun to part sun. Plant in shade if summers are hot a:
dry. Thrives in moist soil but also does well in average ga
den soil. With plenty of moisture, the leaves of some forr
can reach 5 ft. or longer. Plant divisions in the spring or so
seeds thickly in pots or a nursery bed. If foliage needs ne:
ening, clip it back in a long crew cut, about 4–5 in. fro
ground level. Propagate by division; if seed heads develop, t:
plant may self-sow.

■ *elata* 'Bowles' Golden'
(*Carex elata* 'Aurea'; *C. acuta*; *C. flava*; *C. stricta* 'Bowle
Golden')
Bowles' golden sedge, golden sedge
Zones 5–9. P/Cl
Height: 24–36 in. Spread: 24–36 in.

Like a patch of warm sunshine, this golden clump of ge
tly arching foliage lights up the edge of any water garden. T:
$1/8$–$1/2$-in.-wide leaves are sunny yellow with green edges
spring, deepening to a greener hue by late summer. The pla
flowers in late April to June, but it's the foliage that steals t:
show. Said to have been discovered by E. A. Bowles in t:
North Broads, an expanse of wet meadow near Cambrid;
England, it was first named 'Aurea' and is still known by th
cultivar name in England.

In wet soils, this water-loving sedge may spread into :
enormous clump that reaches more than 4 ft. wide. Plant se
eral clumps for a spectacular show and spotlight the effe
with green-leaved bog plants.

ow to Grow

ll sun to part sun. Wet to very moist soil. Thrives in shal-
w standing water, but will grow in average garden soil, al-
ough with less vigor. Plant divisions in spring. Water deeply
times of drought. Propagate by division.

nigra p. 127
ack-flowering sedge
ones 4–8. P/Cl
eight: 6–9 in. Spread: 6 in.

These soft, low clumps of narrow gray-green foliage make
good ground cover, but they spread slowly. Like many
dges, they retain some green leaves throughout the year.
ew foliage emerges in spring from the old leaves, which re-
de into a mulch among the plants. Thrives in very moist
il and is good along the edge of a garden pond or pool. The
usual flowers are thick black spikes atop bare stems, held
st above the foliage.

California black-flowering sedge *(Carex nudata)* is a simi-
r species with taller, even showier flowers, but it mellows to
wny gold and orange in winter. In the West, this sedge is
undant in lush, moist meadows, where it grows with
asses of red and yellow monkey flowers, snapdragon-like
ants that adapt easily to life in a garden.

Both sedges offer contrast to pastel-colored astilbes and
her perennials. Try them in combination with glossy-leaved
rgenias or the tall spears of golden *Iris pseudacorus,* or play
their gray-green leaves with other silvery plants, such as
lerman's Pride' lamiastrum.

ow to Grow

ght shade (*C. nutans* also thrives in full sun). Very moist to
ggy soil, even shallow water. Plant divisions in spring. You
n let the old foliage die back, or you can cut it back in early
ring for a neater look. Propagate by division; plants may
so self-sow.

petriei p. 127
warf brown sedge
ones 7–9. P/Cl
eight: 4–6 in. Spread: 6 in.

This diminutive grasslike plant is another curiosity of the
dge family, with warm brown foliage year-round. Once you
ccept the idea that a living plant can be brown, you'll be
armed by this one. Its tendrils of very thin leaves grow in
upright, arching tuft. The flowers never reach above the
liage and add a curly effect when they mature. It's a pretty

contrast to taller blue-gray grasses, such as blue Magella grass *(Agropyron magellanicum),* which thrives in the mois well-drained conditions that the sedge requires.

How to Grow
Full sun to shade. Moist but well-drained soil. Work lots organic matter such as compost, leaf mold, or aged manu into the soil so that it stays moist and fluffy but doesn't g waterlogged. Plant seeds in pots, then transplant to garde or plant divisions in spring. Water generously during d times.

■ *plantaginea* *p. 128*
Plantain-leaved sedge
Zones 4–9. P/Cl
Height: 12–24 in. Spread: 8–12 in.
    Shade gardeners can enjoy this easy-to-grow sedge as a alternative or a companion to the usual hostas and othe shade ground covers. Its flat leaves can reach an inch wic and look something like the common narrow-leaved plantai weed, except that they grow in a clump instead of flat to th ground. The typical spiky sedge flowers are blackish brow and appear in early spring, held well above fresh green leave The foliage stays green into winter and needs no cutting back
    The bright green, grassy foliage is an appealing accent i the shade garden. Use it to liven up a bed of deep green per winkle or to make a hosta planting look new again with good contrast of color and texture. Also beautiful with fern: Solomon's-seal, Jacob's-ladder, celandine poppy, and othe shade-loving plants.

How to Grow
Light to heavy shade. Moist to average garden soil. Plant d visions in spring. Mulch thickly with chopped dead leave: Water generously during hot, dry summers. If leaf tips brow excessively during drought or hot weather, trim them off wit scissors. Seeds itself when conditions are similar to those c its native Eastern deciduous woodlands.

■ *siderosticha* 'Variegata' *p. 128*
Creeping variegated broad-leaved sedge
Zones 5 or 6–9. P/R
Height: 12–24 in. Spread: 12 in. or more
    A striking foliage plant, this sedge sports broad grass: leaves with bold white edges that light up a shady garden The foliage grows in a continuous sweeping colony rathe than in clumps, spreading by underground stolons, but it : easy to keep in control by hand pulling. You can use it as :

ot accent, or let it spread into a ground cover. Try it along
pathway, where the delicate coloring can be admired up
ose, or use it to highlight a background area of the garden.
ew shoots are pink when they emerge. Foliage turns golden
n in winter.

ow to Grow

ght to medium shade. Moist, rich soil. Plant divisions in
ring. Water frequently during dry summers. Cut back in
inter or early spring. Propagate by division.

texensis

atlin sedge, Texas sedge
ones 7–10. P/R
eight: 3–4 in. Spread: 6 in.

A native of Texas, this evergreen sedge may be the low-
aintenance lawn grass of the future. It's tough and adapt-
ble, staying green even under heavy foot traffic. If you don't
ind a slightly looser look than typical lawn grass, Catlin
dge can be just the ticket for creating a greensward. Because
doesn't need mowing, it's also perfect between stepping-
ones or as a background for flowering bulbs. Try it as an
verplanting for tomasina crocuses, dwarf daffodils, Greek
nemones, and other small bulbs, or for the taller varieties of
affodils. The sedge flowers appear in early spring, but
ey're inconspicuously held against the leaves.

low to Grow

un to medium shade. Adaptable to most soils, from very
oist to drier-than-average garden soil, and will even grow
shallow standing water. Plant in light or part shade in areas
ith very hot, dry summers, such as the Southwest. Plant di-
isions in spring, or for large areas, look for plugs of Catlin
dge, available from lawn-grass suppliers. You can also start
eds in pots, sowing thickly. The sedge needs no cutting
ack, though you can mow occasionally for a neater look in
lawn. Propagate by division or by seed; the plants self-sow
allowed to set seed, and they have naturalized outside Los
ngeles and in some other areas of California.

Chasmanthium

Kaz-man'thee-um
Gramineae. Grass family

Perennial grasses that form clumps or small patches, with
niquely flat seed heads that dangle over the broad leaf
lades. Only five species native to eastern North America.

■ *latifolium* p. 129

Northern sea oats, spangle grass, wild oats

Zone 4. P/Cl/W

Height: 3–5 ft. Spread: 2 ft. or more

  Easy to grow and shade-tolerant, this clump-forming grass makes an excellent ground cover on slopes or open woodland; smaller clumps can accent a pathway or add contrast to a perennial border. The close-set leaves are broad for grass, green in summer and fall and warm tan in winter. The flat, drooping clusters of oatlike seed heads sway above the leaves in the slightest breeze and look wonderful in winter when displayed against a fence or snow. They last in dried arrangements for more than a year. Spreads fast (by seed) in wet sites, less invasive in dry conditions.

How to Grow

Sun or shade. Looks best in full sun and moist, fertile soil. Tolerates poor or dry soil and heat. Sow seed or increase by division in spring; space 2 ft. apart for mass plantings. Cut back to the ground in early spring.

Coix

ko´icks

Gramineae. Grass family

  Tall, branching annual and perennial grasses with flat leaves and abundant flowers springing from the leaf axils. The large, round seeds of some species are used for food and ornament in Southeast Asia. About four species, all of them native to Asia.

lachryma-jobi *p. 129*

Job's tears

Zones 9–10. PGA/W

Height: 3–6 ft. or more. Spread: 12 in.

This old-fashioned curiosity has been grown for centuries in western gardens and even longer in its native Southeast Asia. Perennial in very mild climates, it can easily be grown as an annual from seed in cold-winter areas. The plant is tall and floppy. With a jointed stem and 1½-in.-wide, 2-ft.-long leaves, it looks almost like corn, and like corn it is neither running nor clump-forming. It usually reaches about 3 ft. tall in the garden but can stretch to 6 ft. Many gardeners consign it to the cutting garden because the seeds are valued more than the ungainly form.

The unusual seeds are shaped like big droplets of tears, which gives the plant its botanical and common names (*lachryma-jobi* translates directly as Job's tears). The nutritious seeds are ground for sweet-tasting meal in some parts of the world. They're also popular for beaded necklaces and clothing decorations, and they've been grown at monasteries since the 14th century for use in rosaries. As the seeds ripen, they turn hard as wood and become beautifully colored — shining white or marked with black, soft gray, or violet, all on the same plant. They ripen at various rates, and the drooping flower clusters may still be blooming or fading when other seeds are mature. They fall off the plant when thoroughly ripe.

How to Grow

Full sun. Fertile, moist but well-drained soil. Easy to grow from seed, but start indoors in pots about eight weeks before the final spring frost date. Transplant to garden after soil has warmed, about corn-planting time.

Cortaderia

Cor-ta-dee′ree-a

Gramineae. Grass family

Perennial grasses that form huge clumps of slender, arching, sharp-edged leaves. Feathery plumes on woody stalks rise in the center of the clumps. About 24 species, native to South America and New Zealand.

selloana *p. 130*

Pampas grass

Zone 7. P/Cl/W

Height: 8 ft. or more. Spread: 8 ft. or more

Tough as nails but very showy, this grass makes a huge bi
lowing clump of slender leaves that rise up through the cen
ter and arch over to the ground; foliage is nearly evergreen i
Zone 9, turning tan in colder zones. Cotton candy–like flov
ering plumes on stiff stalks lift 2 ft. or more above the foliag
in late summer and remain showy through midwinter. Fema
plants are showier than the males. It is most often used as
single specimen in mid-lawn but is perhaps better as a barrie
hedge or wind screen, because it gets quite big and the le
edges are dangerously sharp. 'Rosea' and 'Rubra' have pin
plumes. 'Pumila' is a dwarf with flower stalks only 6 ft. ta

The taller species, *C. jubata,* or purple pampas grass, ha
become an unwelcome invader in California and other mil
areas. (Marin County, California, has banned the sale of seec
considering the plant a noxious weed.) Although still widel
offered by nurseries and mail-order catalogs, it's best to avoi
planting it and increasing its already strong roothold i
America's wildlands. Unfortunately, the difficulties of sortin
out pampas grasses, which are variable when grown fror
seed, means that less-careful nurseries still offer this specie
under the name "pampas grass," which more correctly be
longs to its better-behaved relative, *Cortaderia selloana.*
self-sowing is a problem in your area, it's best to avoid thes
grasses altogether and plant the noninvasive native *Muhlen*
bergia rigens instead.

How to Grow
Full or part sun. Grows anywhere; not fussy about soil or wa
tering. Space 10 ft. apart for mass plantings. Remove ol
plumes in spring. Cut back old foliage every few years i
early spring. Use a gas-powered trimmer with a metal blade
burning it off is an easier solution if allowed in your area
Wear gloves and be careful when working around the sharp
edged leaves. Propagate by division.

■ *selloana* 'Andes Silver'
'Andes Silver' pampas grass
Zones 6–10. P/Cl/W
Height: 5–7 ft. Spread: 5 ft. or more
More cold-hardy than many cultivars, this stunning pam
pas grass has billowing plumes of silky, silvery white. Fev
perennial flowers can hold their own against such magni
ficence. Luckily, the orange and red blaze of fall foliage be
gins just in time to match the blooming season of these splen
did grasses. The mass of grass leaves and flowers also look
great with brightly colored winter-interest shrubs, includin
red-twig and yellow-twig dogwoods and red-barked willows

How to Grow
Same as *Cortaderia selloana*.

selloana 'Pumila' *p. 130*
Dwarf pampas grass
Zones 8–10. P/Cl/W
Height: 4–6 ft. Spread: 3 ft.

A plant 3–5 ft. tall isn't usually called a dwarf, unless you're talking about the giants of the pampas grass family. The clumping, arching foliage of this cultivar usually reaches about 3 ft. tall, with the showy plumes carried about 2 ft. above the leaves. Although the plant is smaller than other pampas grasses, the plumes are close to full size. The cultivar blooms in late summer with so many fluffy, erect plumes that it appears a solid mass of golden floss. Dwarf pampas grass often pushes up a few plumes of flowers the first season after planting. It's a gorgeous partner to Japanese maples and right in scale with dwarf mugo pines. Although some catalogs suggest the plant is cold-hardy to Zone 7, it may freeze in cold winters.

How to Grow
Same as *Cortaderia selloana*.

selloana 'Silver Comet' *p. 131*
'Silver Comet' pampas grass
Zones 7–10. P/Cl/W
Height: 6–8 ft. Spread: 6 ft.

This tall cultivar has variegated leaves striped with white, a showy effect even before the plant is in bloom. The platinum plumes are gorgeous with the orange foliage of mountain ash, the scarlet of shining sumac, and the deep black-green of spruces. Like other pampas grasses, it benefits from a dark backdrop that offsets the spectacular flowers. Evergreens, such as spruces, firs, and hemlocks, and purple-leaved shrubs such as 'Royal Velvet' smokebush, work magic with pampas grass.

How to Grow
Same as *Cortaderia selloana*.

Cymbopogon
sim-bo-po´gun
Gramineae. Grass family

Perennial, mostly clumping grasses of the tropics, most of them with highly aromatic foliage that yields an oil widely

used in cooking, perfumes, and herbal medicines. Includes th
plant called nardus *(Cymbopogon nardus),* the source of ci
ronella oil, which is used as an insect repellent. The genus i
cludes about 30 species, native to India, Ceylon, and othe
tropical regions of the Old World.

■ *citratus* *p. 131*
Lemongrass
Zones 9–10. P/Cl/W
Height: 2–6 ft. Spread: 12–24 in. or more

   Cooks and tea drinkers know this plant better than ga
deners, thanks to its wonderful lemon fragrance and flavo
which is used in herb teas and cooking, especially in South
east Asian recipes. The plant is also attractive, and its fres
lemon scent is as delightful in the garden as it is in th
kitchen. Lemongrass will survive the winter only in warm cl
mates, but it makes a beautiful single-season plant in an
area. It grows fast into a clump usually about 3–4 ft. tall an
rarely flowers outside of its native home. The foliage spring
from bulbous-looking stems, which are often colored a prett
reddish purple. New growth also may have this purplish hue
The 1–1$\frac{1}{2}$-in.-wide leaves are soft to the touch.

   Plant lemongrass along a walkway where you can pick
bit of leaf as you walk by. Rubbing the leaf between you
fingers releases the delicious scent. It thrives in containers,
good choice for cold-winter areas because you can easil
move the plant indoors when frost threatens. If your lemor
grass does get killed by cold, cut off the foliage with scissor
and twist it into a fragrant decoration for the kitchen. T
make tea, snip a tablespoon of fresh leaves and steep in ho
water for 5 minutes; add honey to taste.

How to Grow
Full sun to part shade. Average garden soil. Grows well in
pot, but it's a thirsty plant and needs frequent watering; if th
soil dries out completely and the foliage dies, cut it back fo
new growth. If you grow it in the garden in cold-winter areas
slice off a division in late summer and pot it up to bring in
doors in fall. Several weeks in a container outside will allov
the new plant to get established in its pot. Keep on a sunn
windowsill and replant in the garden after the soil is warr
in midspring. Propagate by division.

Cyperus

ý´per-us
Cyperaceae. Sedge family

Annual and perennial plants usually with bare stems topped by an arching cluster of leaflike bracts that open like an umbrella, giving the genus its common name, umbrella sedge. Some sprout true leaves from the base of the plant. Generally, annual umbrella sedges have fibrous roots; perennials grow from rhizomes, which spread, but not fast enough to be called "running."

Most of the 600 or so species are tropical and subtropical natives, from South Africa and Madagascar among other homelands, but some, including the pesky lawn weed called yellow nut sedge *(C. esculentus)*, are naturalized in North America. The unusual form of the plant is eye-catching in the garden. Tender species also make good container plants, especially in and around water gardens, and can be lifted and stored in a protected place in cold-winter areas. Some umbrella sedges are grown as houseplants.

albostriatus
(C. diffusus; C. diffusus 'Elegans'; C. elegans)
Broad-leaved umbrella plant
Zones 9–10. P
Height: 6–24 in., but usually 18–20 in. Spread: 18–24 in.

A beautiful perennial that adds tropical grace to a shaded garden with moist soil. Soft, leafy bracts, to ¾ in. wide and 5 in. long, form a broad umbrella atop the stems. Delicate umbels of fine tan spikelets rise from the center of the canopy like a small, airy bouquet. True leaves at the base of the clump may grow as tall as the flowering stems. The plant spreads slowly from a woody rhizome.

Originally from South Africa, this sedge grows best in damp, shady places, which makes it a perfect companion for hostas and ferns. It's also striking with orange-red impatiens in a pot or in the garden. Like other umbrella sedges, it looks great along the water. 'Variegatus' is an appealing variegated cultivar with understated cream to yellow or lime-green striping along the leaves.

How to Grow
Part to moderate shade; moist to wet soil. Thrives in fertile soils, but also grows in average soil. Does well in humid climates. Dig and divide the rhizomes to propagate. Foliage is interesting in arrangements as well as in the garden. Grow the plant in pots in the water garden, but don't totally submerge the roots.

■ *alternifolius* *p. 132*
Umbrella plant
Zones 9–10. P
Height: 18–36 in. Spread: 18–36 in.

This adaptable perennial sedge grows in a dense clump o
tall bare stems crowned by drooping umbrellas of leaflik
bracts. Dark green like the stems, the bracts are usually abou
a half-inch wide or less and reach as long as 10–12 in., giv
ing them an elegant, spidery look. The smooth, leggy stem
remain uncluttered by true leaves at the base, and sprays o
small flowers top the bracts. The plant expands slowly fron
rhizomes.

Originating in the marshes of Madagascar, Mauritius, an
other islands, umbrella plant is found throughout the tropic
and subtropics. It's a natural in a garden setting near wate
or with bog plants, but it can also be a centerpiece in a moist
soil garden or in a container, and it makes an interesting
houseplant.

How to Grow
Sun to part shade. Must have at least moist soil; thrives i
shallow water and in wet soils. Excellent pond plant sub
merged in a tub. Grows best in fertile soil. Sun and wind i
hot climates will burn the foliage, making it turn brown. Th
bracts will turn brown if nipped by temperatures lower tha
32°F; the root will die in cold below about 15°F. Snip of
brown tips to neaten its appearance. In a serious case of sun
or windburn, or if the plant is touched by frost, cut the dam
aged stems to the ground, give the plant a dose of liquid fer
tilizer, water well if not growing in wet soil, and watch i
push up new stalks. In cold climates, winter the plant indoor
in a well-lit area. Set the pot in a tray of water or on we

avel, and mist frequently to boost humidity. Easiest propa-
tion is by division, but you can also grow from seed or try
oating the inflorescences upside down on water; they may
rout new shoots.

papyrus p. 132

pyrus, Egyptian papyrus, Egyptian paper reed

ones 9–10. P

eight: 6–15 ft. Spread: 3 ft. or more

The first paper was made by pressing the pithy stems of
is plant into a corrugated surface suitable for decorating.
ome suggest papyrus is also the "bulrush" with which
loses' cradle was disguised. Aside from these useful possi-
lities, papyrus is an artistic accent in any garden. Its thin,
readlike bracts, up to 18 in. long, create a profusion of
immering, arching sprays atop bare stems an inch or two
ide. The small flowers turn into brown nutlike fruits that
ot the center of each spray. This is a big plant but an airy
ne. It makes an elegant showpiece for the water garden or
ne patio. Combine with water lilies, lotus, and other plants
ith big, simple leaves for contrast.

'Mexico' is a slightly different cultivar introduced to the
alifornia garden trade. It has denser heads than the species,
anks to an interesting trait of the bracts: each emerges
ngly from the umbel, then splits into two threads about
-12 in. from the center, giving the plant heads an excep-
onally lush look. An individual cluster can be 18–24 in. in
ameter.

ow to Grow

ull sun or part shade. In soil that is constantly very moist,
r in water up to 3 ft. deep. Grow potted in pool and ponds
r plant in earth-bottom water gardens; settle a potted plant
n supporting bricks or stones in the bottom of a large,
ater-filled container for patio use; add a few minnows from
bait shop to keep down mosquito larvae. Clip off any past-
eir-prime seed heads or broken stems. To propagate, divide
ae knotted rhizomes (try a sharp spade or hatchet), or grow
om seed. Floating inflorescences may sprout new shoots.
he beauty of this plant is worth the trouble of overwinter-
ag in cold areas, but its size makes a greenhouse or sunroom
lmost a must.

profiler p.133

C. isocladus; C. papyrus 'Nanus')

warf papyrus

ones 9–10. P

eight: 12–36 in. Spread: 12 in. or more

Like an impertinent young cousin, this umbrella plant has a livelier, less refined attitude than other members of the family. Instead of drooping gracefully, its bracts stick up like hedgehog's bristles. The brushy umbels of bracts are glossy light to medium green, and usually about 3–4 in. across. At 2–3 ft. high, the plant is a miniature when compared to the 15-ft. true papyrus. It's a good scale for a small pool or aquarium. Try dwarf papyrus with red-leaved cannas along the water; its texture and color will liven up the staid, broad leaves of the cannas.

How to Grow

Part shade or light shade. Wet, fertile soil or in water. Prevent drying out; without water, plants may go into a sharp and often irreversible decline. Good container plant, but insert the plastic planting pot into another container filled with water. As umbels go to seed and brown, clip them off to keep the plant looking fresh and green. Easiest propagation is by dividing the creeping rhizomes. You can also grow from seed or float the inflorescences upside down on water to try sprouting new shoots.

Dasylirion

Das-i-leer´ee-on
Agavaceae. Agave family
Woody-based perennials with very short or sometimes medium-height trunks topped with dense clusters of long, slender, often spiny-edged leaves. The rounded leaf base is called a desert spoon. About 18 species native to the Southwest and Mexico.

■ *texanum* p. 133
Sotol, bear grass
Zones 8–10. P/Cl
Height: 2–3 ft. Spread: 3 ft. or more
A rounded mound of spiky leaves 2–3 ft. long and $\frac{1}{2}$-in. wide radiates from the stubby trunk of this perennial like a giant pincushion. The short trunk may be totally underground, so that the plant looks like a clump of grass from a distance. Older plants spread underground to form a clump of rosettes. Leaves are medium to dark green with yellowish spines along the margin. Slender flower stalks up to 15 ft. tall and topped with wormlike clusters of small greenish, yellow, or white flowers arise in late spring and last for several weeks.

The leaves of the plant have been used for thousands of years as thatch and in basketry by native people of the desert ıthwest and Mexico, and the leaf fibers have been turned ₀ string and rope. An alcoholic drink called *sotol* is also de from the plant. Useful for desert gardens, combined ch succulents and shrubs, and interesting in a container ₁t keep away from passersby; the leaves are sharp). Several ₁er species are offered by native plant nurseries.

₁w to Grow

ll to part sun. Needs good drainage. Thrives in hot, dry ·s, unamended soil, and caliche. Remove old bloom stalks. eds no other maintenance.

₂schampsia

s-champs´ee-uh

amineae. Grass family

Clumping, mostly perennial grasses with rough leaves and ısses of delicate-looking flower stalks. About 50 species, ₁st native to cool regions in the Northern Hemisphere.

₁aespitosa *p. 134*

fted hair grass

₁nes 4–9. P/Cl/C

ight: 2–3 ft. Spread: 2 ft.

A North American native and once the dominant grass in ₁untain meadows, this cool-season grass was valued for ·age because it greened up early. The species and several va- ₁ies also occur in the ever-shrinking bogs and wet places ₁m Greenland to North Carolina, west to Illinois and in ₁e western states, and in arctic and temperate areas of the ₁ World. The plant was first valued for garden use in Eu- ₁e, so unless you find a supplier that uses regional plants stock, your tufted hair grass is likely to be of Eurasian ex- ₁ction.

Excellent for mass plantings, tufted hair grass creates a del- ₁e cloud of bloom from late spring through summer. The ₁wers are held in panicles that can reach 5 ft. tall above ₁unds of spiky or arching foliage. They are pale greenish ₁low tinged with purple and ripen to golden tan. Plant the ₁ss against a dark background to show off the flowers to ₁t effect, or use it in a woodland garden where the glisten- ₁ panicles add light and airiness. Foliage is evergreen or ₁ievergreen even in northern climates (it has remained ₁en at temperatures lower than –13°F), so you can also in- ₁de this species in a border of plants for winter interest. Cut ₁wers can be used in fresh or dried bouquets. 'Tardiflora' ₁oms two to three weeks later than the species. 'Bronze

Veil' ('Bronzeschleier') produces a golden brown cloud
drooping panicles that almost hides the foliage. (See photo
p. 134.) 'Gold Pendant' ('Goldgehange') has rich golden y
low clouds of flowers. A single plant is strong enough to co
mand attention in the garden, or you can group them
extra effect. (See photo on p. 135.) Try 'Gold Pendant' alo
water or in a woodland garden with witch hazel, corylops
and other shrubs. Also beautiful with purple-leaved smo
tree, even when the flowers are past their prime. Tufted h
grass also makes a good turf grass in low-traffic areas. In P
ble Beach, California, it is planted on golf course roug
where it goes dormant in late summer but remains attract
as a low, golden, undulating surface.

How to Grow
Part shade or moderate shade. Will grow in sun, but grow
and bloom will not be as good as in shade. Tolerates aci
or alkaline conditions if the soil is fertile and moist. Plan
ft. apart in masses for best effect. Cut flower stalks back
late summer, or let the fine bleached stems stand through
winter. Cut foliage to the crown in early spring (or early su
mer where summers are hot). Cold-hardy but doesn't ta
heat well. A long-lived, unfussy plant. May self-sow. Pro
gate by division or seed. In coastal central California, ba
of this grass are now widely available. The grass is harves
as hay when seeds are mature; to plant, simply spread the h
on the selected area.

■ *caespitosa* 'Holciformis'
(D. holciformis)
Pacific hair grass
Zones 8–9. P/Cl/C
Height: 18–24 in. Spread: 18–24 in.

   This cultivar has the same erect, tufted foliage as
species in a lighter shade of green, but its flowers are very d
ferent. Instead of being carried in light, open, branching pa
icles, they're narrow, slightly arching wands thick w
flowers and then seeds. They mature to a beautiful golden y
low. The grass blooms early and the foliage stays evergre
Other cultivars and the species flag in hot, sunny climat
this one does not.

   Once a common native in marshes, sandy soil, and coas
prairies from Vancouver Island to central California a
along the Big Sur coast, 'Holciformis' has a wilder look th
the species. It is best used in naturalistic plantings, where
bleached panicles will reflect the natural cycle of seasons l
the wild grasses of the mountain foothills.

ow to Grow

n or part shade. Does best in moist soil but will also tol-
ate dry, even sandy, soil. Cut back after flowering for neat-
ss.

flexuosa
ira flexuosa)
inkled hair grass, wavy hair grass
ones 4–8. P/Cl/C
eight: 8–12 in. Spread: 8–12 in.

A delicate-looking but tough little treasure with a tuft of
nder leaves and a bouquet of slim-stemmed flower spike-
s. Purplish or bronze when they emerge in summer, the
florescences mellow to a fine gold that makes a shimmering
ze when backlit by the sun.

Native to dry or rocky woods, slopes, and open ground in
e Northern Hemisphere, it lends a dainty presence to wood-
d gardens and shady borders. It's also beautiful at the top
a slope, where afternoon light can highlight its branching
nicles. Mingle patches of crinkled hair grass with heathers
d heaths, or try it in a planting of shiny-leaved bearberry
rctostaphlyos uva-ursi). In arrangements, fresh or dried, it's
airy as baby's-breath.

ow to Grow

ows best in acidic soil high in humus or other organic mat-
. Does well in moist soil but also thrives in dry shade; tol-
ates drought. Part shade or light to moderate shade; sun in
ol northern climates. Divide to propagate, or start from
d. (Cultivars, except for the golden-leaved 'Aurea', proba-
y will not come true from seed.) May self-sow, cropping up
unexpected niches, especially among rocks.

lymus
h-mus
amineae. Grass family

The wild rye grasses are mostly perennials, tufted or rhi-
matous; some are so vigorously invasive that they are
inted for dune control. About 50 species are included in
e genus, all native to the temperate Northern Hemisphere,
m Russia and Eurasia to Canada, Alaska, and California.
aves are stiff and may be dangerously sharp, especially
e tips.

■ *arenarius* 'Glaucus' *p. 135*
(*Leymus arenarius* 'Glaucus')
Blue Lyme grass, blue wild rye, blue European beach grass
Zones 4–10. P/R/W
Height: 1–2 ft. Spread: 2 ft. or more

The gray-blue foliage of this loose, open grass is so tempt-
ing to include in the perennial border that many gardeners
move it right in despite its well-deserved reputation for ag-
gressiveness. The unearthly blue color combines well with
almost any perennial, especially those with pink, white, or red
flowers. The spiky-looking leaves are surprisingly soft to the
touch; the edges, however, are sharp enough to slice an un-
wary finger. Flowers look like narrow heads of grain.

The native *Elymus glaucus*, or blue wild rye, is a striking
blue-green. The noninvasive plant grows quickly into a tight
bunch with large broad leaves and stems that reach 2–3 ft.
tall. The clump eventually reaches the size of a bushel basket
at the base. It thrives in part shade and does best in moist
soil. Grow from seed.

How to Grow
Highly adaptable. Plant in sun to part or light shade, in any
soil. Thrives in dry conditions. It has a tendency to become
floppy and somewhat open; keep it compact and in good
color by occasionally cutting it back to the crown. Propagate
by division. Unless you're growing the grass for erosion control, contain its spread with sunken barriers or by planting in
a bucket.

■ *condensatus* 'Canyon Prince' *p. 136*
(*Leymus condensatus* 'Canyon Prince')
'Canyon Prince' wild rye, giant wild rye
Zones 7–9. P/Cl/C
Height: 18–24 in. Spread: 18–24 in.

Another superb silvery blue grass, this selection forms a
mound of stiff upright leaves. It spreads much more slowly
than *E. arenarius* 'Glaucus', so it's a better choice for the
perennial border. Also outstanding in foliage gardens or with
shrubs. The narrow spikes of flowers rise to 6 ft. above the
foliage.

How to Grow
A recent introduction, found growing wild along the California coast, this grass's adaptability is still being tested.
Thrives in full sun and in shade, and apparently in most soil,
including heavy clay and sand. Does well beneath oaks. Cut
back when foliage loses its blue color. Propagate by division.

tritichoides *p. 136*
(*eymus tritichoides*)
reeping wild rye, beardless wild rye
ones 7–10. P/R/W
eight: 2–4 ft. Spread: 2 ft. or more

A fast-spreading native grass of the American West, this
een to blue-green species colonizes large areas with its
reading, scaly rhizomatous roots. Inflorescences look like
m heads of grain without the "beard" hairs. Native to
oist soils from Montana to Baja California and Washington
ate, it hybridizes with other wild species; varieties that dif-
r in size, foliage color, and habit are also common. Good
r masses or ground cover; keep it out of the mixed border.
xcellent for controlling erosion on slopes.

ow to Grow

un to part or light shade. Moist to dry soils. Seems as adapt-
le and as tenacious as other species in this genus. Becomes
rmant during periods of drought; cut back and water to
courage new growth. Propagate by division.

quisetum

-kwih-see′tum
quisetaceae. Horsetail family

The 35 or so species of horsetails are primitive plants that
ave remained unchanged since the days of the dinosaurs.
hey have noticeably jointed stems, and some species have
horls of leaves or branches at the joints (which gives the
nus its common name, horsetail). The leafless species look
ke grass from a distance, especially when they spread to car-
t a stream bank or hillside. Related to ferns, they reproduce
y spores, which are formed in small pine cone–like struc-
res at the tops of the stems.

The bare-stemmed species are popular in California land-
aping and around water gardens, although they're adapt-
le enough to grow almost anywhere. Horsetails are found
st about everywhere in the world except Australia and New
ealand.

hyemale *p. 137*
couring rush
ones 5–10. P/R
eight: 18–48 in. Spread: 18 in. or more

A vigorous, erect perennial with cylindrical stems that
rout thickly from creeping rhizomes. At a distance the rush

looks like a swath of tall green grass, but up close you ca
see the plant's interesting jointed stems. The $1/4$–$3/8$-in.-thi
stems are marked at the closely spaced joints with off-whi
bands and black fringes. The stems are loaded with grains
silica, the rough substance that gives the plant its commo
name, scouring rush. Native Americans used it to scrub coo
ing vessels and showed European settlers how to do the sam
Some used the plant fresh; others burned masses of it an
used the high-silica wood ashes as a scrubbing powder. If yo
grow this interesting plant, you can give it a try yourself –
a bundled-up handful of stems works better than a plast
pad on glass casserole dishes or the outdoor grill (but keep
away from Teflon).

In its native haunts, scouring rush usually grows in w
places or along water and in the East can often be four
growing near winterberry holly (*Ilex verticillata*). Excelle
beside pools and in bog gardens; it is also a common lan
scape accent and planter subject in southern California. Th
simple upright form looks great in a large clay or decorate
pot and its spare lines are used to complement modern a
chitecture. The matte dark green stems keep their color a
year, which makes this a good plant to grow in mass for wir
ter interest. Add a clump of tawny miscanthus for a lovely v
gnette in the snow.

How to Grow

Sun to shade. Almost any soil, from waterlogged clay to dr
sandy soil. Plants are shorter and slower to spread in dr
soils. Colonizes by creeping rhizomes; keep it in place wit
barriers of plastic buried 10 in. or deeper and pull up any e
rant roots. Cut back dead brown or gray stems as needed c
let them fall naturally. The silica-loaded stems will dull you
pruning shears in just one session, as if you'd been cuttin
through sandpaper. Propagate by division.

■ *scirpoides* var. *contorta*

Contorted dwarf scouring rush, miniature contorted horseta
Zones 6–10. P/R
Height: 2–6 in. Spread: 6 in. or more

This unusual little horsetail has stems as thin as fine wir
and as gently curved as a head of wavy hair. The textur
makes you want to reach out and pat the plant. The stem
are dotted with the typical light bands at the joints. Th
niceties of this miniature are best appreciated at close rang
so try it in a pretty container on a patio table, or spotlight
between stones along the edge of a pool.

How to Grow

In to light shade. Moist to wet soil of average to rich fertility. Will also thrive in shallow water. Don't let this one dry out; it has a hard time recovering from a dry spell. Rhizomes creep slowly to expand the plant but are easy to control if needed. Slice off pieces with a sharp trowel to propagate.

Eragrostis

er-uh-grahss´tis

Gramineae. Grass family

The beauty of many of the species in this large genus is reason enough for the name love grass, a direct translation of the botanical name, *Eros* for love and *agrostis,* a grass. The genus includes some 250 annual and perennial grasses, widely distributed in North and South America as well as Eurasia, Australia, and Africa. Habit varies from mounding perennials to lax, crabgrasslike annuals. Some love grasses provide valuable forage in difficult conditions; the rigid stems of *E. obtusiflora,* for instance, have gotten many an animal through hard times in the dusty, alkali soils of the West.

curvula p. 137

Weeping love grass

Zones 7–10. P/Cl/W

Height: 12–24 in. Spread: 18–24 in

This mounding grass is a common sight along roadways in Arizona, Texas, Florida, and other mild-winter states, but it actually comes from the mountains of Tanganyika. Introduced in the 1920s to the South and Southwest by the U.S. Department of Agriculture to control erosion and revegetate grasslands, it slipped the bounds and is now part of the naturalized flora. Not nearly as pushy as other U.S.D.A. mistakes, weeping love grass is beautiful, with fine, flowing texture like a mane of hair in a shampoo commercial. The dark green foliage turns reddish tan, then straw-colored in winter; it stays evergreen in climates without frost. Arching, open panicles of delicate flowers rise above the clump in fall; look closely and you can see the wavy undulations of the panicle branches that give the plant its botanical name. Plant on slopes, where you can appreciate the flowing form of the foliage, in the perennial border or a mixed-grass planting. Its relaxed attitude also looks good along a wood fence or stone wall.

How to Grow

Sun. Grows well in almost all soils as long as they are w
drained. Thrives in sandy soils; exceptionally drought-tole
ant. Cut back old foliage in early spring. Self-sows in m
climates. Start from seed sown in pots or propagate by div
sion.

■ *spectabilis*
Purple love grass
Zones 5–9. P/Cl/W
Height: 12–18 in. Spread: 6–18 in.

In late summer and early fall, a cloud of soft reddish pu
ple covers the plant like a haze of smoke along the groun
It's hard to believe that a single small tuft produces enou
hazy bloom to span a 3–4-ft. area. The gauzy effect is cr
ated by fine-stemmed, many-branched panicles of delica
flowers. After the seed heads mature and drop, the spe
flower heads often break off and roll along the ground li
tumbleweeds. This grass is beautiful in the border or
masses. Try it with dwarf pink or white zinnias and ta
grasses, or with late-blooming perennials, such as sedum 'A
tumn Joy', blue mistflower (*Eupatorium coelestinum*), purp
coneflowers, or New England asters.

How to Grow

Sun. Average to light soils; must be well drained. Excellent
sandy soil. Also grows well in clay, as long as it doesn't sta
waterlogged. Give it space; don't overcrowd. Usually doesn
need cutting back — old foliage dies back in spring as ne
growth pushes out — but you can neaten it up if neede
Start from seed; it may self-sow. Propagate well-establishe
plants by division.

■ *trichodes* 'Bend'
'Bend' sand love grass
Zones 5–9. P/Cl/W
Height: 2–5 ft. Spread: 1–2 ft.

The glossy leaves of this fine-textured but substantial gra
rise in tufts, then bend sharply at the top. In summer, fin
branched, arching panicles emerge in a cloud of shimmerin
pinkish bronze. The flower heads are so profuse they ma
spill over, eventually making the plant weep and sometime
collapse. A circular wire support set halfway up the foliag
before bloom will help the grass hold its head up. Plant as
single specimen in a mixed perennial border, or in group
The flowers make a graceful bouquet in a slim vase.

How to Grow

un. Average soil. Semievergreen; cut back before new growth egins in early spring. Propagate by division or seed. Self-ows in mild-winter areas.

Erianthus

ir-ee-an´thus
Gramineae. Grass family

Perennial grasses with tall reedy stems, flat spreading leaf lades, and silky flowering plumes. About 20 species, native o temperate and tropical climates. Some botanists now combine *Erianthus* with *Saccharum,* the genus that includes sugar ane.

ravennae p. 138
(Saccharum ravennae)
Ravenna grass, plume grass, hardy pampas grass
Zones 6–10. P/Cl/W
Height: 9–12 ft. Spread: 5–6 ft.

A dramatic grass for large landscapes, ravenna looks a lot ike pampas grass *(Cortaderia selloana).* Its flower plumes, up o 2 ft. long, last from September through winter, lightening rom purplish to beige to silver. Cut them to use for fresh or ried arrangements. The pleasantly fuzzy stalks hold plumes vell above 1-in.-wide leaves, which are soft on top but like andpaper underneath. Although big, this plant is not inva-ive — it forms a clump and doesn't spread. Keep the mature

size in mind when placing it in the garden; beside a patio o
next to a narrow walkway it would be overwhelming, but i
makes a good screen or backdrop for a border. You'll enjo
its constant movement and rustling sound on breezy days. I
mild climates, it may self-sow and spread beyond the garden
it has become naturalized in Arizona.

How to Grow
Full sun. Best in relatively infertile, dry soil, where it stays up
right and strong; requires staking in fertile or moist condi
tions. Cut old stalks to the ground in early spring. Propagat
by division or start from seed. May self-sow.

Eriophorum

air-ee-o′for-um
Cyperaceae. Sedge family
   The cotton grasses are neither grasses nor cotton, but the
are still well named. All bear the signature tufts of fluff
white flowers from which the genus gets its name (*erion* i
Greek for wool). The genus includes about 30 species of an
nual and perennial grasslike plants, usually evergreen, whic
may grow in clumps or spread by rhizomes. Floating on cot
tony fibers, the seeds are quick to colonize damp marshes and
bogs. Native to the north temperate zone and the Arctic, cot
ton grasses are a common sight on the tundra; they languish
in warm climates.

■ *latifolium*   p. 138
Cotton grass
Zones 4–8. P/Cl/W
Height: 8–18 in. Spread: 12 in.
   This charming grasslike perennial bestows a sense o
humor on the garden. Its white cotton balls emerge in spring
and dance across marshy sites like the tails of a hundred
Easter bunnies, making them irresistible to kids and olde
garden visitors alike. The thin, spiky leaves grow in erec
clumps, and the plant forms colonies by self-sowing. Try cot
ton grass in a naturalized wet meadow or along the edge o
a pond.

How to Grow
Sun. Moist or wet acidic soil that mirrors native bog condi
tions; will also grow in average garden soil if watered fre
quently. Best in cool climates. Propagate by seed or divide es
tablished plants. May self-sow.

Festuca

ess-too´kuh

Gramineae. Grass family

Many popular ornamental grasses and valuable lawn and forage grasses belong to this genus of over 300 perennial species. They occur throughout the world but are most abundant in temperate and cold regions including Eurasia, North Africa, and North America. They are generally clumping plants with some tall and coarse-bladed, such as *Festuca elatior*, or English bluegrass, a commonly grown pasture grass. The ornamental types are usually springy tussocks or mats of fine, wiry foliage, often blue-gray in color; they are beautiful and useful, but unfortunately, mostly short-lived.

A note on nomenclature: Like many other grasses, fescues are often sold under different botanical names for the same plant, and identification is often confused. Alternative names are listed in the descriptions that follow. Many of the ornamental cultivars developed in Germany are listed in catalogs by their German names; some suppliers use English translations. Both are provided in these plant descriptions.

amethystina   p. 139

(*F. ovina* 'Glauca')

sheep's fescue, tufted fescue, large blue fescue

Zones 4–8. P/Cl/C

Height: 8–12 in. Spread: 12 in.

A cool-season evergreen grass that grows in weeping clumps of very fine foliage, usually of a blue-gray cast. Panicles of dainty flowers are deep gray-blue at first and ripen to golden tan and beige. It's at its best in spring, and it languishes in summer humidity.

The plants grow in neat tufted mounds, perfect for edging a bed or pathway. They can also be combined with perennials such as cottage pinks and catmint in a mixed border, or grown close together as a ground cover, though they won't last much beyond three years and will need replacing as they decline. Cultivars offer improvements on the species; try 'Bronzeglanz' ('Bronze Glaze' or 'Bronze Luster') for showy flowers and bronze-hued foliage, or 'Klose', an olive-green fescue with extra-fine texture and blue-colored new growth. 'Superba' has excellent blue-gray color and purple-stemmed flowers that ripen to tan; clip them off if you don't care for their color against the foliage.

How to Grow

Sun; light shade in hot-summer climates. Light, moist but very well drained soil. Cut back after flowering if plant looks shabby. This is a short-lived plant. Propagate by division or by seed.

■ *gautieri* *p. 139*
(*F. scoparia*)
Bearskin fescue
Zones 4–6. P/Cl/C
Height: 4 in. Spread: 4 in.

The dense, bright green clumps of this fescue form nea[t] cushions that invite patting — but beware. The leaves will ja[b] you like a million needle pricks. The deception is no reaso[n] to avoid growing it. The tight mounds are ideal for carefull[y] maintained rock gardens or troughs of alpines, where this na[-] tive of the Pyrenees will feel most at home. It's a charmin[g] companion to dwarf columbines. The cultivar 'Pic Carlit' i[s] a more compact variety.

How to Grow
Part to moderate shade. Average to dry soils. Extremel[y] drought-tolerant. Though tough, this little grass demands per[-] fect drainage and does best in cool conditions. Give the plan[t] several inches of bare space around it and lighten the so[il] with plenty of gravel. Propagate by careful division.

■ *glauca* (*see below for photos*)
(*F. ovina*, *F. ovina* 'Glauca', *F. ovina* var. *glauca*, *F. cinerea*)
Blue fescue, blue sheep's fescue, gray fescue
Zones 4–9. P/Cl/C
Height: 8–18 in. Spread: 8–12 in.

The versatility of this grass makes it one of the most pop[-] ular ornamentals. Fine, wiry leaves form a dense cushion o[f] striking blue-gray that combines well with plants of all col[-] ors. The species gets its name from the word "glaucous," re[-] ferring to a thin gray coating on the leaves that rubs off a[s] easily as the bloom on grapes. Blue fescues are cool-seaso[n] grasses, which means most of them go dormant in summe[r] heat. Some cultivars hold their color even in hot weathe[r.] Most are evergreen (or "everblue") in milder winters.

The list of synonyms above testifies to the confusion o[f] classification of these grasses. The simplest solution for th[e] gardener, if not the botanist, is to ask for the named cultiva[r] (see the list on the facing page), which will give you the bes[t] chance of getting the plant you want, regardless of whethe[r] it is classed as *Festuca cinerea*, *F. glauca*, or something else.

Use groups of blue fescue between flowering perennials i[n] the border to intensify pinks and other pastels, to highligh[t] whites, cool down hot reds and oranges, or separate color[s] that might clash, such as salmon and bubblegum pink. Tr[y] them with grasses of contrasting color, such as red-leaved cul[-] tivars like 'Warrior' switch grass (*Panicum virgatum* 'War[-] rior') and flame grass (*Miscanthus sinensis* 'Purpurascens'[).]

hey also look great with coarser gray-leaved grasses, including blue oat grass *(Helictotrichon sempervirens)* and Heavy Metal' switch grass (*Panicum virgatum* 'Heavy Metal'). When other grasses are cloaked in winter colors of wheat and straw, the cool gray cushions of blue stand out like mirror reflecting the sky.

Fine texture and regular shape make blue fescues a good hoice for edging borders and paths, accompanying small onifers and alpine perennials in rock gardens, and covering mall patches of ground. Planted in mounds about 8–10 in. part, they create a look like a billowy gray sea. They are ill uited, however, for steep hillsides or other sites that are not asily accessible. The plants keep a distinctly mounded form hat makes weeding around them necessary, and their short ife span (usually three years or less) means that older specimens must be replaced as they expire.

How to Grow

Sun; light to part shade in hot-summer areas. Very well drained, average to fertile soil. Best in areas without high ummer humidity. Drought-tolerant. Cut back when plant ooks shabby or the mound loses its compactness. An annual arly spring haircut, to 3 in. above the crown, will keep plants looking fresh and new. Many go dormant in summer; cut back to crown and they will regrow when cooler weather ind moisture return in fall. Keep a fresh supply of plants by aking small divisions from established clumps each spring. If he mound dies out in the center, dig up, slice into sections, ind replant.

Propagate by division or seed. Division will ensure the ame traits as in the parent. If you're the adventurous type, ry growing blue fescues from seed. They won't all look the ame — some will be taller, others shorter; some mounded, others more erect; some blue, some green.

As blue fescue has gained in popularity, the number of cultivars on the market has skyrocketed. The following are particularly noteworthy; German names are given in parentheses. All thrive in Zones 4–9 and can be grown as described below. Unless otherwise noted, all grow upwards of 8 in. high ind wide.

'Blue Glow' ('Blauglut') is outstanding among fescues for its intense blue-gray foliage. On the small side, it grows to 6 in. high and wide and holds up well to summer heat.

'Blue-Silver' ('Blau Silber') is another excellent silvery blue cultivar that almost glows in the garden. It stays beautiful even in hot summers. One of the best for eastern and midwestern summers. (See p. 140.)

'Elijah's Blue' is one of the palest cultivars, with foliage of light silver-blue. It makes a striking companion to strong-co-ored flowers, such as deep purple *Campanula glomerata* c Siberian iris 'Caesar's Brother', or with brilliant red Orient: poppies. (See p. 140.)

'Sea Urchin' ('Seeigel') is a very fine textured, springy clum of green rather than blue-gray foliage. An interesting accer in a perennial border or edging, it also makes a good groun cover. (See p. 141.)

'Solling' doesn't flower and is therefore a good choice fo those who like the foliage effect of blue fescue but find th flowers distracting. The beautiful clump of fine leaves feel like soft steel wool to the touch, and the plants knit togethe into an almost seamless turf if placed closely.

'Tom Thumb' ('Daeumling') makes a dainty tuft about 4 ir high and 4–6 in. wide. New growth is soft blue-gray-greer changing to green with maturity. It's good for an accent in small-scale garden or for an edging.

■ *muelleri* *p. 141*
Mueller's fescue
Zones 5–9. P/Cl/C
Height: 6–8 in. Spread: 6–8 in.
   This cool-season perennial grass grows in soft, fine-tex tured mounds of thin, wiry foliage. It's one of the best greer fescues for the garden and occasionally may show a touch o blue-green in certain light. A more erect but coarser green fes cue is *F. mairei*, Moroccan fescue.

How to Grow
Like *F. glauca.*

Glyceria
glih-seer´ee-uh
Gramineae. Grass family
   The deliciously sweet seeds of the species *Glyceria fluitan* have given the genus its common names sweet grass and manna grass. These good-tasting forage grasses, including G elata, a native grass of the moist Northwest woods, fow manna grass *(G. striata)*, and others, are like candy to duck. and other waterfowl, who seek them out in moist meadow. and other wet places. The 16 perennial species in this genu:

ail from Australia, New Zealand, South America, and the
orthern temperate zone, most of them native to marshes and
hallow water.

Many manna grasses are tall and reedlike, but they vary in
abit, and their flowers can be narrow spikes or large, open,
ranched panicles. Most spread by creeping rhizomatous
oots. They are excellent plants for wildlife gardeners, but
nly the species below is commonly sold in the ornamental
rade.

maxima (see below for photo)

Manna grass, reed sweet grass, reed manna grass
Zones 5–10. P/R/W

Height: 2–6 ft., usually 2–3 ft. Spread: 4 ft. or more

This tall, reedlike perennial grass spreads by rhizomatous
oots to form large stands. The $1/4$–$1/2$-in.-wide leaves are
ong and coarse in texture, but the large panicles of flowers
ave a delicate grace. An aquatic grass that grows well in
hallow water or wet soils, it's a good plant for large ponds,
vhere it holds its own along the water's edge with other aggressive plants like cattails (*Typha* spp.) and yellow flag iris
Iris pseudacorus). It may be too unruly for small, restrained
vater gardens.

Variegated manna grass ('Variegata') is a bright-colored
ultivar. (See p. 142.) New foliage emerges with a pretty pink
int, then changes to ivory and then to yellow, with green
tripes becoming noticeable in summer. The plant has a ca-
ually erect-arching habit, with leaves bending over near the
ips or at various heights. It's a fast spreader, so give it space
vhere it can grow en masse.

How to Grow

Sun. Moist to wet soil or in water (to 2 ft. deep); also grows
n average moist garden soil, where it is less inclined to
pread. Think before you plant; this is a fast mover and
difficult to get back in bounds. Propagate by division.

Hakonechloa

1ah-ko-neh-klo´uh
Gramineae. Grass family

This genus includes only a single species, a graceful,
preading mound of arching foliage most familiar to gardeners in its golden-variegated form. These slow-growing plants
are expensive, but if your budget allows, they make a gor-

geous ground cover. Hakonechloa grows in the wild on th
Japanese island of Honshu, where it finds a roothold on th
rocky cliffs and spreads by creeping stolons.

■ *macra* *p. 142*
Hakonechloa, hakone grass
Zones 4–10. P/Cl/W
Height: 12–30 in. Spread: 24 in. or more
   This perennial Japanese forest grass is rich green in its nat
ural species form. The loose, spilling foliage is so beautifu
that the fine-seeded fall inflorescences are almost an after
thought. It has the quality of an elegant, low-growing bam
boo for shade gardens, setting off the wide leaves and forma
habit of hostas with its flowing grace. Its smooth leaves tur
rusty orange-bronze in autumn, a beautiful effect with fall
blooming witch hazels or with the flaking bark of river
birches or parrotia.

How to Grow
Part to moderate shade; shade in hot-summer regions. Mois
but well-drained, humusy soil. Water generously when rain
fall is scarce. A beautiful plant worth the bit of extra troubl
to make it happy. Spreads very slowly by creeping roots
Grows taller in cool climates. Cut back old foliage when
needed. Propagate by division.

■ *macra* 'Aureola' *p. 143*
(*H. macra* 'Urahajusa Zuku')
Golden hakonechloa, golden hakone grass
Zones 4–10. P/Cl/W
Height: 12–24 in. Spread: 18 in.
   Many gardeners would rate this the most beautiful orna
mental grass of all. Its lovely golden leaves spill over from
their wiry stems like a waterfall, not just in a single mound
but in a series of cascading sprays that give the plant a fluid
motion. The buttery yellow leaves are slightly streaked with
green. In fall their color intensifies to pink, at first just at the
tips and edges, but eventually the whole plant is a rich, warm
pink-red. Let this grass carry the show in a shade garden by
partnering it with the green foliage of hostas, ferns, and other
shade lovers. It looks beautiful with rock, too.

How to Grow
Same as *H. macra*. Less robust in growth than the green
species, it is even slower to spread. If it begins to turn more
green than yellow, move it to a sunnier spot.

Helictotrichon

ell-ik-toe-try´kun

Gramineae. Grass family

These clump-forming perennial grasses have arching leaf blades and rather sparse flowers held in narrow panicles. The genus includes about 30 species, most native to Eurasia, and a species native to alpine meadows and dry western prairies of North America.

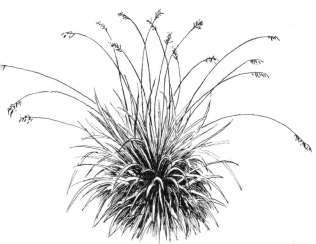

sempervirens p. 143

(Avena sempervirens; A. candida)

Blue oat grass

Zones 4–9. P/Cl/W

Height: 12–36 in., usually about 24 in. Spread: 12–24 in.

This clumping perennial is the same bright blue as blue lyme grass (*Elymus arenarius* 'Glaucus') but is much better behaved in the garden. The spiky leaves are thin, only $\frac{1}{8}$–$\frac{3}{8}$ in. wide, and grow in dense tufts like a large version of blue fescue *(Festuca glauca)*. It doesn't flower much, especially in cold climates, but from the minute the leaves emerge in spring its foliage is an eye-catcher. Combine it in a foundation planting with a dwarf blue spruce and one of the dwarf blue-colored junipers, or contrast it with perennials of different habits and leaf shapes. Like other blue-gray grasses, it looks great with pink garden flowers.

How to Grow

Full or part sun. Needs well-drained soil to perform well, especially where winters are wet. Does best in a hot, sunny site. Develops the best blue color in dry soil. Pull out dead leaves as necessary, and cut back once a year. Divide older clumps in spring.

■ *sempervirens* 'Saphirsprundel' *p. 144*
'Saphirsprundel' ('Sapphire Fountain') blue oat grass
Zones 4–9. P/Cl/W
Height: 24 in. Spread: 24 in.

Like the species, but with even better clear blue-gray col
Its gently arching panicles rise above the stiff, evergreen leav
in late summer. A superb grass for the perennial border,
ther as a single accent or in groups as a transition. Try it wi
garden phlox of any color; white phlox will shine behind
planting of this cool-colored grass, which will also camo
flage any mildewed foliage. This grass has extremely shar
tipped, stiff foliage; work around it with care.

How to Grow
Same as *H. sempervirens.*

Hordeum

hor´dee-um
Gramineae. Grass family

These annual or perennial grasses have showy, brist
flower heads that can be highly ornamental in mass plan
ings. The genus includes about 20 species native to the nor
temperate zone, including the cereal grain barley *(Hordeu
vulgare)* and many aggressive weedy grasses. The sha
flower spikes can be a danger to foraging animals, piercin
mouths, eyes, and noses.

■ *jubatum* *p. 144*
Foxtail barley, squirreltail grass
Zones 4–10. PGA/C
Height: 12–30 in. Spread: 12–18 in.

A short-lived grass often grown as an annual for cut-flow
arrangements or massed in informal gardens. It's utterly bea
tiful for several weeks in early summer when the feather
flower heads emerge. The nodding spikes are 4 in. long, a
each floret is topped with a hairlike 3-in.-long awn. T
flowers have a green and purple sheen that turns to beige
the "tail" puffs out and matures. Pick early for dried arrang
ments; discard any that show signs of falling apart. If yo
don't harvest or cut back the seed heads before they shatt
the grass will probably self-sow and may become weedy. Ne
ther clumping nor running, foxtail barley grows like whea
single-stemmed and lots of it.

This North American native is considered a pesky and da
gerous weed in irrigated western pastures because the brist

eds can injure foraging animals. If you live near grazing
nd, ranchers will thank you for not introducing it.

ow to Grow

ll or part sun. Not fussy about soil or watering. Plant seeds
spring and grow as annual. Harvest or cut back seed heads
fore they shatter to prevent grass from self-sowing.

Hystrix

´stricks

ramineae. Grass family

The botanical name of this genus is Greek for porcupine,
apt description for these grasses, whose seed heads bristle
all directions like porcupine quills — or like the bristles of
bottlebrush, their common name. They're perennials with
ose tufts of leaves, and all share the typical bristly seed
ad. The six species are native to North America, China,
ew Zealand, and India.

patula p. 145

ottlebrush grass

ones 4–9. P/Cl/W

eight: 24–48 in. Spread: 12–24 in.

This perennial American native is an interesting plant for
shady garden, thanks to its trademark bottlebrush seed
ads, which persist from late summer through fall. In its natal haunts from Nova Scotia to North Dakota and south to
eorgia, it occurs in and at the edge of woods. The foliage is
iremarkable; the loose, upright tufts of $\frac{1}{4}$–$\frac{1}{2}$-in.-wide leaf
ades bow near the top in a curly jumble, but above the
aves rise erect stems of bristled flower heads that catch the
ght, and the eye, in a shaded garden. The flower heads hold
eir florets close to the stem at first, but later open so that
e bristles stick out at right angles. The flowers start green
d ripen to beige above green leaves, which follow suit in
te autumn. The grass makes an interesting counterpoint to
e blue spires of the shade-loving American bellflower *(Cam-
nula americana)*. For fresh arrangements, cut the flowers
hen they first emerge.

ow to Grow

ll sun or part to moderate shade. Widely adaptable.
hrives in heavy clay as well as humusy soils and dry, rocky
ade. Easy to grow from seed. Best for the naturalized gar-
n. May self-sow and will readily populate a well-kept gar-
n. Propagate by seed or division.

Imperata

im-per-ah´tuh
Gramineae. Grass family

A small group of perennial grasses, mostly from tropic
climates. Of the eight species, one is a fast-spreading creep
ing grass, *I. cylindrica*, that was introduced to Florida as
forage grass. It is now classified as a noxious weed and ca
not be sold in this country. A cultivated form of this gras
with striking red foliage, is a treasured ornamental.

■ *cylindrica* 'Red Baron' *p. 145*
(*I. cylindrica* var. *rubra*)
Japanese blood grass
Zones 6–9. P/R/W
Height: 12–18 in. Spread: 12 in.

Not as robust as the species, the mild-mannered 'R
Baron' is a welcome addition to the garden. It seldom if ev
flowers and is grown for its bright red foliage. Leaves becom
flushed with garnet red as summer progresses, darkening in
burgundy toward fall. Use it for an accent plant, especial
on a west-facing lawn or ridge where it will be backlit by t
setting sun. It also makes a colorful ribbon running along
lawn or edging a perennial border.

How to Grow
Full or part sun. Best in fertile, moist but well-drained so
Propagate by division. Cut back once a year. If all-gree
shoots appear, it's a sign that the cultivar is reverting to
species type. Remove and destroy them immediately.

Juncus

jun´kus
Juncaceae. Rush family

Rushes have been appreciated for their usefulness
thatch, cordage, sandals, baskets, and other everyday prod
ucts far longer than they've been admired by gardeners. The
botanical name has its root in the Latin *iugere*, to join, r
ferring to the use of the stems in weaving and tying. In Japa
soft rush (*Juncus effusus*) is still cultivated for tatami, t
woven mats that cover the floors of Japanese homes. The
plants are also useful to animals in the wild. They are the f
vorite food of muskrat and moose and other creatures th
frequent marshes, bogs, and other wet places. Ducks and m
grating swallows seek out heavy stands of rushes for prote
tive shelter. In the garden, rushes add a natural look to wat
features, blurring the transition from water to land.

effusus p. 146
(*Juncus communis*)
soft rush, common rush, mat rush
Zones 4–9. P/Cl
Height: 18–48 in., usually about 24 in. Spread: 18–30 in.

This wayfaring rush occurs around the globe. Usually found in wet soil near water, it also grows in rich lowlands that are periodically flooded. Early European settlers in North America soon learned that the presence of this plant meant that the ground was too wet to cultivate crops.

The thin, cylindrical stems are dark green, almost black-green, and grow in a dense clump that spills outward from an erect center. The clump gradually expands by creeping roots. The foliage has a stiff look, but its stems are soft to the touch, and its flowers are a pretty addition. They sprout several inches down from the tips of the stems in nodding clusters of soft brown or gold. Each seed capsule contains innumerable minute seeds that look like dust. Soft rush makes an attractive plant in shallow water or at the edge of a pond. It turns golden in fall, then beige-brown in winter. Horizontally banded cultivars are available: 'Aureostriatus', with yellow bands; 'Vittatus', with narrow white bands; and 'Zebrinus', with broad white bands.

How to Grow
Sun to part or light shade. Grows most lush in rich, moist or wet soils or in shallow water, but is very adaptable. Tolerates dry soil in summer, but some stems may turn brown. Cut back old foliage in early spring, or let new stems grow up through old. May self-sow. Propagate by division; you can also grow from seed, but division yields a bigger plant faster.

effusus 'Spiralis' p. 146
(*J. effusus* var. *spiralis*)
corkscrew rush
Zones 4–9. P/Cl
Height: 12–24 in. Spread: 12 in. or more

A curiosity for the water garden or container, this cultivar has curling stems that writhe every which way, like Medusa's hair. Clip some for arrangements and let the rest serve as a conversation piece or private poolside joke. The cultivar 'Curly Wurly' has even tighter spirals.

How to Grow
Part to light shade. Moist or wet soil; also shallow water. If you want to try it in a container, plant in a plastic pot and insert into a nondraining container filled with several inches of water, or keep on a saucer of water-filled gravel. Propagate by division.

■ *patens* p. 147
California gray rush
Zones 8–9. P/Cl
Height: 18–30 in. Spread: 18 in. or more

This rush has the typical spiky, cylindrical clump of stem but it holds them more stiffly erect than soft rush. The flowe are brown bumbles held within the clump of stems. The fo liage is a variable blue-gray-green and keeps its color yea round.

How to Grow

Sun to moderate shade. Very adaptable, but at its best i moist or wet fertile soil. Will also grow in shallow water. Ma be hardier than Zone 8; it hasn't been tried much outside o its native West Coast. Propagate by division. May self-sov Cut back old foliage as needed.

Koeleria

koe-lair´ee-uh
Gramineae. Grass family

About 25 species of annual and perennial grasses with tuf of slender leaves and narrow spikes of flowers from the tem perate regions of the Northern and Southern Hemisphere Although the common name for the genus is hair grass, th coiffure varies considerably: some species are dense and lu trous, like a well-combed mane, and others look more like cheap Beatles wig. Most grow in upright tufts. Some hav blue-gray foliage. All are cool-season grasses that sport wand of showy flowers in late spring to summer, when the perer nial garden is at its peak. Most of the ornamental specie have a short life, lasting only one or two years in the garder

■ *argentea* p. 147
Silver hair grass
Zones 6–9. P/Cl/C
Height: 12–18 in. Spread: 12–18 in.

Thick clumps of fine-textured, $\frac{1}{8}$–$\frac{1}{4}$-in.-wide leaves hav a silvery cast that is more pronounced on the undersides o the leaves. This gives the plants a shimmering look, especiall when they move in the breeze, like the flashing undersides o silver maple. The greenish white panicles of flowers bloo about the same time as Oriental poppies and irises and ar smooth and glistening when they first emerge. They ripen t golden tan, still ornamental, although some gardeners prefe to clip them off so as not to detract from the grass's foliag They are pretty flowers for dainty bouquets. Originally fror the Himalayas.

ow to Grow

un. Lean soils with excellent drainage. This grass sulks in
hade, clay, and wet soils, but must have some moisture, al-
hough it is fairly drought-tolerant. A short-lived species that
arely lasts more than a couple of years in the garden. Cut
ack dormant foliage and wait for new cool-season growth.
ropagate by seed or division.

glauca *p. 148*
(*K. cristata* var. *glauca*)
arge blue hair grass
ones 6–9. P/Cl/C
Height: 6–24 in., usually about 12 in. Spread: 6–12 in.

Dainty next to most grasses, it grows in a dense mound of
hin leaves that flash blue-gray. Wands of flowers cover the
lant for several weeks in late spring to summer. The clump
hay include mature whitish tan panicles as well as glossy
reen ones just emerging.

How to Grow

ame as *K. argentea*. This small grass is easy to fit into a
erennial border, although it will be short-lived in the moist,
ertile soil usually found there. It does best in infertile, sandy,
lkaline soil.

macrantha *p. 148*
Crested hair grass, June grass
Zones 2–9. P/Cl/C
Height: 12–18 in. Spread: 12 in.

This tufted perennial grass grows in erect, compact clumps.
ts leaves are usually tinged with gray-green, although the in-
ensity of the color may vary. The narrow spikes of flowers
rovide good vertical line, especially when the grass is used
n mass plantings. Since it self-sows readily, it's best to keep
t out of the border. Plant it in a naturalistic meadow, with
wildflowers like black-eyed Susans and yarrow, or put it in a
roup with other grasses. It also looks good with native west-
rn drylands plants, such as artemisias and desert marigold,
r with Mediterranean herbs, including oregano and billowy
lue catmint.

How to Grow

un. Lean, light soil with excellent drainage; rocky or grav-
lly soil. Thrives in drought and intense sun, but declines in
moist, fertile soil and in shade. A good grass for a naturalis-
ic western desert landscape. Cut back if dead foliage is dis-
greeable to you, or let new green leaves come up through
he old clump. Scatter seed for a meadow planting, or prop-
gate by division. Self-sows.

Lagurus

la-gur´us
Gramineae. Grass family
The only species is described below.

■ *ovatus* *p. 149*
Hare's tail
All zones. A/W
Height: 12–24 in. Spread: 6–12 in.

The oval panicles of this annual grass are as white and furry as bunny tails. (The genus name comes from the Greek *lagos,* hare, and *oura,* tail.) The soft foliage is also a pleasure to stroke, but the loose tuft of green leaves usually goes unnoticed once the flower heads spring up. Plant this summer bloomer in your annual garden with wiry-stemmed red field poppies or with stout, colorful zinnias, or grow it for cutting. Clip the flowers when young for long-lasting decorations in dried arrangements. Plant grows like wheat: lots of single stems.

How to Grow
Sun. Light, very well drained soil; also does well in average garden soil. Sow seed in spring where you want the plants to grow. Self-sows but never to pest status.

Luzula

loo-zoo´luh
Juncaceae. Rush family

In the same family as the familiar pond and marsh rushes, the 80 or so species in this genus are mostly native to woodlands rather than wet places. Their flat, grasslike leaves are often soft and hairy, and they grow in tufts or loose, low mounds. In the wild they look just like clumps of grass among the leaves of the forest floor. All perennials, they are good, underused plants that deserve more attention in the shade or woodland garden. They combine beautifully with violets and spring ephemeral wildflowers as well as the more usual hostas and ferns. Most are native to Eurasia, but some are native to North America, and others are naturalized here.

■ *nivea* 'Snowbird' *p. 149*
'Snow Bird' snowy wood rush
Zones 4–9. P/Cl
Height: 8–12 in. Spread: 8–12 in.

The showiest of the wood rushes, this perennial bears abundant clusters of lovely white flowers above its thin gray

ves. The clump of foliage is soft to the touch, thanks to
e velvety hairs on the leaves, which collect dew in shining
ver droplets along their edges. 'Snow Bird' looks great
ainst the deep tones and round leaves of ornamental foliage
ucheras such as 'Palace Purple' and 'Pewter Veil'. The
ecies form of this cultivar has ivory-colored flowers that
ature to soft beige and is beautiful with wild blue phlox
hlox stolonifera and *P. divaricata*).

ow to Grow

rt to light shade. Best in moist, humusy soil. Propagate
om division, or grow from seed (not all seedlings will be ex-
tly like the parent cultivar). Cut back spent flowers and fo-
ge as needed.

Ielica

el' ih-kuh

ramineae. Grass family

Melic grasses are tall clumping grasses, medium to fine in
liage texture, with varying types of inflorescences. Some are
rrow and dense, others are soft and fluffy or strictly one-
led, and some have shimmering, open panicles with a light,
ythmic beauty. The 60 or so species, all perennials, hail
om Eurasia, North Africa, and other temperate regions.
any are western North American natives. The genus name
obably refers to the sweet sap of *Melica nutans* and may
me from the Italian *miele*, meaning honey.

altissima 'Atropurpurea'

rple Siberian melic

ones 4–9. P/Cl/C

eight: 8 in. Spread: 8 in.

The cultivar name of this clump-forming, cool-season
rennial refers to the flowers, not the foliage. Its $3/8$–$3/4$-in.-
ide leaves are green, with a slight gloss, and grow in a low
ump. Flowers arise on tall bare stems that can quiver as
uch as 2 ft. above the foliage, with delicate, open panicles
at take on a tawny purplish hue. The species is from
beria, and this cultivar has an innate preference for cool cli-
ates and an aversion to hot sun and dry soil. Try it in a
ghtly shaded or moist-soil perennial border or in a shade
rden. Because of its low foliage, you can use it as a see-
rough plant; its slender flowering stems won't obscure
ants behind it. The delicate, early-blooming flowers are
arming with salvias and other small-flowered perennials.

How to Grow
Part shade; keep it out of direct sun in hot-summer region
Moist, humusy, very well drained soil; dig in a generou
amount of compost, leaf mold, or rotted manure to lighte
heavier soils. Cut back spent flowering stalks and dorma
foliage. Self-sows, but seedlings may not be like the pare
plant. Propagate by division.

■ *ciliata* *p. 150*
Hairy melic grass, silky spike melic
Zones 5–8. P/Cl/C
Height: 8–12 in. Spread: 8–12 in.

   This perennial cool-season grass grows in tufts of gra
green foliage, but you'll never notice the leaves once th
flowers appear in late spring or early summer. The cylindr
cal spikes are pale, creamy tan, with silky white hairs as sof
looking as down. Erect at first, they settle into a slight nod
ding posture. They are just as decorative in arrangements a
in an informal garden, where the flowers can lean about in
casual way and collapse comfortably. If you want them t
stay at attention, wrap a circlet of wire around them.

How to Grow
Sun to part shade; keep out of full sun in hot-summer area
Moist but well-drained soil of good fertility. Cut back afte
the flowers are spent and the foliage is dormant. Propagat
by seed or division.

Milium
mil´ee-um
Gramineae. Grass family
   The flat-bladed leaves of the annual or perennial mill
grasses grow in medium-tall relaxed tussocks. Only one of th
six species in this genus is grown as an ornamental, and usu
ally in the yellow variegated form. In its species form, it
found in moist or rocky woods from Nova Scotia to Min
nesota and south to Maryland, as well as in Eurasia.

■ *effusum* 'Aureum'
Golden wood millet, Bowles' golden grass
Zones 6–9. P/Cl/C
Height: 12–24 in. Spread: 12–24 in. or more
   This cool-season perennial grass has glorious yellow-gree
foliage that spills over in an arching mound of flat, $1/4$–$1/$
in.-wide leaves. It spreads at a slow to moderate rate b
creeping roots but is never a pest. Planted in shade or

-ooded setting, golden wood millet lights up the garden like
 pool of sunlight on the woodland floor. The young leaves
ave the strongest yellow coloring; they become green-yellow
s the season progresses. When backlit by afternoon sun, the
anslucent foliage comes alive. Delicate open sprays of
owers rise well above the grassy foliage in late spring to
arly summer and quiver in a shimmering haze with every
reeze. After flowering, the plant may decline a bit. The fo-
age is evergreen in mild climates.

Bowles' golden grass is beautiful with the usual ferns and
ostas, but for something special, try combining it with the
uttery cupped flowers and deep green foliage of celandine
oppy *(Stylophorum diphyllum)* and the flowering, bare
rown branches of yellow Cornelian cherry *(Cornus mas).*

low to Grow

ight to moderate shade. Moist but well-drained, humusy soil
ch in organic matter; also does well on a rocky, woodsy
ope and adapts to average garden soil in shade. Cut back
pent flowers and tired foliage. To propagate, slice off divi-
ons with a sharp spade or start from fresh seed; most of the
eedlings will come true to color. May self-sow moderately.

Miscanthus

nis-kan´thus
iramineae. Grass family

The premiere genus of ornamental grasses, and rightly so.
Infussy about soil and conditions, these robust perennials

grow in sturdy clumps, providing backbone in the landscape and adapting to a multitude of uses, from hedges to poolside greenery to specimen plantings. Some have wide banners of leaves; others finer, arching foliage. All sport showy plumes of flowers that can persist for months in the garden and even longer in dried arrangements. It's a pleasure to watch the flowers emerge and mature; they have a satin gloss and often beautiful pink, red, or purple coloring when new, and then gradually soften to fluffy heads delightful to touch. Even when the seeds have blown away, the bare, curled stems of the inflorescence remain appealing. In the winter garden, miscanthus grasses add structure and beauty, as well as delightful rustling noises and movement.

There are 17 species of miscanthus, but dozens of fine cultivars have been selected. These versatile grasses are native to the Old World tropics, Southeast Asia, and South Africa. Many ornamental cultivars have been developed by plant breeders in Germany. Some ornamental grass suppliers list the plants by their German names; others use English translations. Where appropriate, both are provided in these plant descriptions.

■ *floridulus*   *p. 150*
(*M. sinensis* var. *giganteus*; *M. japonicus*)
Giant Chinese silver grass
Zones 5–9. P/Cl/W
Height: 8–12 ft. or more. Spread: 36 in. or more.

A big grass, sometimes misidentified as M. 'Giganteus' with arching leaves up to $1\frac{1}{2}$ in. wide and stout stems up to 2 in. in diameter. Stems grow strongly erect from the base of the clump and hold the grass upright even in wind. The flowers appear in early to midfall and are a bonanza in areas with long growing seasons. They're silky at first, with a reddish sheen, and then feather out into fluffy pyramidal plumes held a foot or more above the foliage. Like all miscanthus flowers, they're beautiful in fresh or dried arrangements. The grass goes dormant in fall. The leaves first turn purplish red over tan, then gradually drop from the culms by midwinter, leaving a structural accent of vertical stems.

This giant can be the center of attention in a mixed border or grouping. Its lush foliage complements other large plants, such as plume poppy (*Macleaya cordata*), cup plant (*Silphium perfoliatum*), and hibiscus, including the wild red mallow (*Hibiscus coccineus*). It also makes a good hedge or windbreak and is a fine anchor for a group of mixed grasses. Leaves tend to die off near the base of the plant, leaving it with a bare-legged look. If you find this unappealing, plant shorter grasses.

How to Grow

Sun. Moist but well-drained soil. Reaches its best height in moist soil, but adapts to average garden conditions. Consider the site carefully before you plant; this tough-rooted grass will soon be impossible to remove without the aid of heavy equipment. Stays in a very slowly enlarging clump. Cut back old stems in early spring; by summer, it will be a dense waterfall of wide green leaves.

oligostachyus
(*M. oligostachys*)
small Japanese silver grass
Zones 5–9. P/Cl/W
Height: 3–4 ft. Spread: 2 ft.

This Japanese native is as diminutive as a miscanthus gets, being only knee-high. It's also less dense, growing in narrow, vertical clumps that need no staking to stay in good form. Its erect flowers, a beautiful pinkish silver, are borne in late summer. It's a good grass for a place of honor in the perennial border, and an attention-getter in groups or in masses. Combine it with 'Purple Dome' fall asters and other late-blooming perennials of contrasting mounded form, or carpet the ground at its feet with low-growing lamb's-ears. The grass mellows to soft tan in winter.

How to Grow

Sun. Well-drained average garden soil. Cut back old foliage in early spring. Propagate by division.

sacchariflorus *p. 151*
silver banner grass
Zones 5–9. P/R/W
Height: 4–8 ft. Spread: 2–3 ft. or more

Unlike most, this miscanthus species grows by creeping rhizomes, spreading especially fast in wet areas. This grass is a native of wetlands in Japan, China, and other places, and it's happiest in moist soils. That makes it an excellent choice for edging a pond or adding interest to a wet meadow. It has wide leaves, up to $3/4$ in. across, that thrust strongly upward and then arch over. The late-summer flowers are soft silver when they emerge and fluff out to white whiskbrooms; they're a little narrower than the spreading feathery flowers of the familiar *M. sinensis,* and they stand upright, well above the foliage. Like other miscanthus flowers, they can tell you at a glance which way the wind blows, since they eventually stiffen in a posture with the plumes turned away from prevailing winds. The grass turns warm yellow to golden tan in fall and winter, and the flowers stay attractive for months.

How to Grow

Sun. Moist to wet soils. In dry soils or clay, it spreads mor[e] slowly and isn't as lush. Choose a site carefully; it is aggre[s]sive. Keep it out of perennial borders, and plant it where [it] can roam. Cut back old foliage in early spring. Propagate b[y] division.

■ *sinensis* (see below for photos)
Eulalia grass, Japanese silver grass
Zones 5–9. P/Cl/W
Height: 3–12 ft., depending on cultivar. Spread: 3 ft. or mor[e]

The old man of ornamental grasses, Eulalia has been [a] garden favorite for centuries. Ancient clumps still thrive i[n] front of American Victorian houses. This warm-season peren[n]nial grows in large clumps. Its leaves grow up then out, in [a] cascade of graceful foliage. The flowers are a superb secon[d] act. They arise in summer to fall, gleaming like silk, then fluf[f] out into showy sprays above the foliage. The grass turns var[i]ous shades of gold and tan in fall, with occasional russe[t] overtones. Its foliage holds up well even in snowy climates.

Adaptable and versatile, this grass grows well in almos[t] any garden and in most combinations. Dense foliage make[s] it a good backdrop for perennial flowers, and it adds pizzaz[z] to plantings of shrubs and evergreens. It's a standard in wa[terside gardens and in mixed-grass groupings. A row or grou[p] of miscanthus also makes a neighbor-friendly hedge.

Dozens of easy-to-grow cultivars are now available, an[d] new ones are appearing all the time. The listings here includ[e] many of the long-time favorites, as well as a sampling of th[e] best new cultivars. Unless otherwise noted, the cultivars grow well in Zones 5–9.

ow to Grow

n; will also grow in part shade but tends to be floppy there.
verage soil. Cut back old foliage in early spring. Propagate
y division, if you can; these plants are tough-rooted and
any cultivars are hard to divide even with an axe.

luetenwunder' forms a tight, erect clump that reaches about
ft. Foliage is strongly vertical, not arching significantly even
the tips. Small plumes of flowers bloom in late summer. Be
reful working around this grass; the leaf edges are sharp
ough to slice an ungloved hand. It is hardy to Zone 4.

urgunder' ('Burgundy') is a slim miscanthus that grows to
ft. The thin, curling leaves give it an airy look, and their
usual deep-red flushed color is beautiful with pink or yel-
w perennials as well as with white-flowered phlox, salvias,
d with annuals such as multiflora petunias. Zones 7–9.

abaret' is a tall (6–8 ft.) variegated cultivar with cool green
d white foliage. The broad ribbons of almost inch-wide
aves, white in the middle with green edges, grow in a weep-
g cascade. 'Cabaret' blooms in early fall, with straight stems
f pink flowers that lighten to soft creamy white. Foliage
rns tan in winter. Variegated forms of miscanthus are ele-
ant with white-flowering perennials, but they also look good
ith almost any other color. They're particularly effective
artners for blazing reds. Try this grass with scarlet salvia
alvia splendens) or shrublike, red-flowered pineapple sage
. elegans), or let it add a cool backdrop to a raised pot of
aming red geraniums. It grows in Zones 7–10. (See photo
n p. 151.)

osmopolitan' is a variegated cultivar of imposing stature
anks to its girth of 4–5 ft. and broad leaves that spill over
ke a handful of wide ribbons. From a distance, the foliage
oks cool gray-green; up close, you can see that the effect is
reated by white edgings on each green leaf. Abundant
lumes of flowers emerge coppery red and are held high
bove the foliage. This is a fabulous specimen plant that
eeds no staking and is excellent in warm climates. (See photo
n p. 152.)

lamingo' is a lush, elegant grass with huge pink plumes. Put
in a place of honor as a specimen or along water, where its
irrored image can double the glory. (See photo on p. 152.)

old Feather' ('Goldfeder') has foliage of an unusual lime
reen edged with gold bands. Less robust than most cultivars
ut worth patience until it's large enough to make a splash.
rows 5–6 ft. tall.

'Gracillimus', or maiden grass, is one of the most delicate cu
tivars but also one of the hardiest (Zone 5). A longtime ga
den favorite, it has narrow leaves that grow in a wide, arc
ing clump up to 8 ft. tall. It may collapse under the weig
of its own foliage and flowers, and it will certainly bow b
neath snow unless you support it with a sturdy loop of wir
It blooms late, in midfall. The silken tassels are rich coppe
red at first and mellow to silvery white. Foliage turns war
tan in winter. (See photo on p. 153.) 'Gracillimus Nana' is
miniature form with even finer foliage. At 3–4 ft. tall,
makes an excellent choice for smaller gardens. Can be slo
to become established.

'Graziella' is a slender-leaved, early-blooming miscanthus th
reaches about 6 ft. high and 3 ft. wide. Large white flower
held well above the foliage, appear in summer. The wic
swords of iris leaves will look even more emphatic beside th
cultivar's slender foliage, and pure white shasta daisies a
lovely with this grass. Hardy to Zone 5. (See photo on
153.)

'Kascade' is an early-blooming cultivar providing a long di
play in Zones 5–8. Growing 5–7 ft. tall and 3–4 ft. wide,
raises its pink flowers in summer, and they soon spill over
their own weight, washing down the plant in a gleamir
wave of silver-pink. It's a glorious plant for the mixed bord
or as a specimen grouping, and it's unbeatable near wate
(See photo on p. 154.)

'Little Fountain' ('Kleine Fontaine') is a compact cultivar
3–4 ft. in height with an extra-long flower show. Rather tha
coming all at once, its blooms push up over a period
weeks, producing a continuous fountain of flowers over th
green leaves. Its compact form makes it an excellent choic
in front of taller grasses or in the mid-ground of the bord
(See photo on p. 154.)

'Morning Light', a relatively new cultivar, is a smaller versio
(4–5 ft.) of 'Gracillimus'. Its silver-striped, fine-textured leav
glisten in the wind, giving it a light, airy feeling in the garde
that's just like the old favorite. In early to midfall, deep pin
bronze flowers push up, then lighten to oatmeal white. It
beautiful by itself or in groups and looks great with the hea
ier branches of woody shrubs, such as 'Arnold Promise' wit
hazel, or with the glossy leaves of bayberry and other broa
leaved evergreens. Light pink wands of coral bells and feat
ery astilbes are enchanting against the shimmery foliage
this grass. Hardy to Zone 5. (See photo on p. 155.)

urpurascens', or flame grass, earns its name in fall, when
e red-tinged foliage changes to a beautiful red-orange. It
lds good color into winter, gradually deepening to bur-
ndy. A compact, upright grower, 4–5 ft. tall, it expands
adually by spreading rhizomes. Grows well in light shade,
ough fall foliage will be lighter and less vivid. Its hardiness
in dispute, with recommendations ranging from Zone 7 as
r north as Zone 4. (See photo on p. 155.) 'Hercules' has a
milar erect habit and warm reddish gold foliage in fall. It
aches 3–5 ft. tall and is hardy to Zone 4. (Both cultivars
ay be listed as *M. oligostachyus.*) Try either of them with a
ump of flaking cinnamon-barked river birch and a bevy of
rple autumn crocus at its feet, or combine with ornamen-
l junipers and other small conifers with interesting color.

arabande' is an excellent hardy cultivar (to Zone 4) similar
the popular 'Gracillimus', with finely textured foliage
uched with silver for an extra-light effect. Contrast it with
mass of deep green coltsfoot *(Tussilago farfara)* at its feet,
plant it in the border with perennials such as hardy gera-
ums, salvias, or glistening pink and white mallows.

ilver Feather' ('Silberfeder') grows to 9 ft. with a spread of
ft. or more and is hardy to Zone 5. Early in the season it
esents a flared arch of fresh green foliage, followed in sum-
er by large plumes of silver flowers held high above the fo-
ge. (See photo on p. 156.)

ilver Spider' ('Silberspinne') is another narrow-leaved culti-
r that tops out at 4–5 ft. The fine-textured foliage has a sil-
ry lightness. In late summer, it blooms with spidery tassels
at are reddish at first and then turn silver. Grows in Zones
-9.

iren' ('Sirene') has possibly the best flowers of any mis-
nthus, raising an abundance of extravagant plumes high
ove the 5–6-ft.-tall foliage. An excellent specimen and beau-
ful along water. Grows in Zones 5–9.

trictus', or porcupine grass, is an old favorite and still valu-
le in today's gardens. (It may also be listed as *M. sinensis*
r. *strictus.*) It flourishes in light or part shade in hot sum-
er climates and will also grow in wet soil or in shallow
ater. It forms a substantial vertical clump (6–8 ft. tall and
–5 ft. wide) of sharply pointed leaves, with some sticking
ut at 45° angles like a pelt of sharp quills. Light yellow hor-
ontal bands mark the leaves with an effect like dappled sun-
ght. New leaves are green and acquire the typical coloring
they mature. This grass is often confused with *M. sinensis*

'Zebrinus', zebra grass, which has the same yellow bands b a habit that is arching and graceful rather than rigidly uprig and prickly. Porcupine grass foliage is interesting in fre arrangements. It quickly turns tan in cold weather.

'Undine' is a slender-stemmed cultivar with pretty silv flowers and warm fall color. It grows to only 4 ft., a goo size in the smaller garden, the perennial border, or as a tra sition between taller grasses and ground covers. Grows Zones 5–9. (See photo on p. 156.)

'Variegatus', one of the oldest variegated cultivars, can st be found in "grandma's gardens," often with another o timer, ribbon grass *(Phalaris arundinacea* var. *picta)*. An ou standing garden grass, it grows to a substantial height a width (6–9 ft. high and 4–5 ft. wide) and has creamy strip foliage that looks ghostly white at a distance. It is beautif in the perennial garden or along water, and the color brigh ens any group of mixed green grasses. Though often plant with black-eyed Susans, its cool color is a better foil for re pink, blue, purple, and white flowers. A nice partner f Siberian irises. Prone to collapse, even without the weight the abundant pink flowers that bloom in early fall; give it sturdy loop of wire for support. Thrives in part or lig shade. Give it some afternoon shade where summers are h Grows in Zones 6–9. (See photo on p. 157.)

'Yaku Jima' looks like a downsized version of *M. sinen* 'Gracillimus'. Not only smaller (3–4 ft.) than other misca thuses, it also has narrower leaves. Abundant buffy flowe bloom in summer and are usually held above the foliage. (S photo on pp. 48–49.) Newer Yaku Jima–type cultivars ha improved on the standard. 'Adagio', one of the most co pact, is perfect for a smaller mixed bed or border. The flowe stretch high above the compact clump, and in fall the leav turn a rich coppery bronze.

'Zebrinus' or Zebra grass, like porcupine grass *(M. sinen* var. *strictus),* has horizontal yellow bands speckling the f liage and grows to the same height (6–8 ft.) but in wide (6 ft.) arching mounds that have a tendency to collapse wit out a little support from the gardener. Young leaves lack t yellow bands at first but develop them as they mature. Fluf pinkish flowers bloom in fall. An old favorite, it's a goo grass for garden or water's edge. (See photo on p. 157.)

transmorrisonensis p. 158
evergreen miscanthus
Zones 7–10. P/Cl/W
Height: 3–4 ft. Spread: 3 ft.

The unusual evergreen habit of this warm-season grass and its small size have some taxonomists arguing for its status as a separate species. Others say it belongs with *M. sinensis*. A recent introduction from Taiwan, it grows in dense arching clumps of narrow green leaves and bears reddish flowers that open to warm tawny gold. It stays evergreen in mild climates and blooms in spring. In cold climates it blooms in early to midsummer. Flowers are held high above the foliage, but cascade out from the plant in an arching curve.

How to Grow
Same as *M. sinensis*.

Molinia
mo-lin´ee-uh
Gramineae. Grass family

These clumping perennial grasses have soft, narrow leaves and loose flower heads. There are only two or three species, native to bogs of Europe and Asia, including the open moors, which is where they get the common name, moor grass. Purple moor grass *(Molinia caerulea)* is sometimes found growing wild in limited areas of the eastern states.

These grasses have never achieved the popularity of the miscanthus tribe, but they're equally valuable in the garden and as carefree, although a bit more persnickety about soil conditions, preferring an acidic soil. Moor grasses are natural companions with heaths, heathers, and Scotch broom, but they also look at home with perennial flowers, shrubs, and conifers. Try them against a dark background to accentuate the delicate flowers, especially when they take on warm autumn tones. Once you discover their beauty, you won't be able to resist adding them to your garden.

caerulea (see below for photo)
purple moor grass
Zones 4–9. P/Cl/W
Height: 1–3 ft. Spread: 2–3 ft.

Don't let this low-mounding grass fool you — when it's in bloom it reaches for the sky, shooting stalks of airy flowers

6–7 ft. into the air. The "purple" *(caerulea)* in the name i[s] little misleading; its only trace is in new flowers, but they m[ay] also be brown or tan, and at any rate, they quickly lose a[ny] purple sheen as they ripen to tawny gold.

This warm-season perennial grass has a bold presence, [yet] because of the see-through quality of the bare flower ste[ms] and airy panicles, it's lightweight enough to use in a mix[ed] border. It also looks dramatic with rocks or on a hillside wi[th] artemisias, perovskia, and other shrublike plants. Or min[gle] a small group of them with heathers.

'Heidebraut' ('Heather Bride') has dense, compact clum[ps] of leaves, and flower stems that mostly stand erect, offer[ing] excellent vertical line with the grace of transparent flowe[rs.] The stems and spikelets are a warm tawny gold in color, a[nd] the flowers are abundant. (See photo on p. 158.)

'Moorflamme' is an outstanding compact cultivar f[or] cooler climates. Foliage reaches 1–2 ft. high and turns orang[e-] red in fall with deeper notes of purple. Its flowers emer[ge] dark purple-brown.

How to Grow

Sun or very light shade. Does best in moist, acidic soil. W[ill] also grow in clay and sandy soil and will tolerate some dr[y-] ness. Foliage and flowers eventually fall on their own, brea[k-] ing off at the base of the stem; clip off any straggling folia[ge] in early spring. This grass requires some patience to g[et] started from a small division; give it two or even three yea[rs] to reach its full glory in the garden. Once it flowers, it m[ay] self-sow, but seedlings take several years to reach a good si[ze.] Propagate by slicing off 4–6-in. divisions from mature plan[ts.]

■ *caerulea* ssp. *litorialis* *p. 159*
(*Molinia litorialis; M. caerulea* ssp. *arundinacea*)
Tall moor grass
Zones 5–8. P/Cl/W
Height: 2–3 ft. Spread: 2–3 ft.

Stalks of this taller version of purple moor grass shoot [up] to heights of 6–9 ft., carrying the flowers like a burst of fi[re-] works above the low-growing foliage. Flowers and folia[ge] turn warm yellow in fall, then soften to golden tan for wi[n-] ter. Like other moor grasses, this tall one's slender flow[er] stalks make it easy to place in the mixed border. They wo[n't] obscure plants behind them or shade those in front.

'Skyracer', an even taller selection, can reach 6–8 ft. wh[en] in flower. Its slim but strong straight stems make it an exce[l-] lent architectural accent in the garden. Turns rich buttery y[el-] low in fall. (See photo on p. 159.)

'Staefa' is a hardier (Zones 4–9) and shorter version of t[all]

oor grass, its flowers reaching only 4–5 ft., roughly half the
ight of the tallest cultivars. The foliage is more weeping in
bit and turns a lovely warm yellow in fall.

One of the most delicate moor grasses, 'Transparent' has
agile flower heads that rise to a hazy cloud at a height of
-6 ft. It is a fine-textured sparkler in the garden or along a
all pool.

ow to Grow
me as *M. caerulea.*

uhlenbergia

ew-len-ber´jee-uh
ramineae. Grass family

These mostly American, mostly perennial grasses differ so
uch in appearance from species to species that only a bot-
ist can tell they're all related. Some are low and creeping,
ith narrow flowering spikes; others are arching clumps with
ouds of flowers. Of the 125 or so species, all but about eight
e native to the West, Southwest, and Mexico; the rest hail
om southern Asia.

Many of the muhly grasses are valuable forage on the
estern range. The recent interest in native American plants,
owever, has made growers and gardeners take a closer look
their ornamental possibilities. With their natural adapta-
on to the rigorous western climate, especially the excellent
ought tolerance of many species, they could become future
rden favorites in the West. As these grasses are tried in gar-
n settings, they may turn out to be adaptable to gardens in
her areas of the country as well.

dumosa p. 160
amboo muhly
ones 8–10. P/R/C
eight: 3–9 ft., usually 3–6 ft. Spread: 3 ft. or more

This unusual grass looks like a miniature fine-textured
amboo. Its leaves start out solidly sheathed around the wiry,
oody stems, then branch and rebranch at the middle and
oper nodes, forming cascades of foliage. The flowers are
orne at the tips of the branches, and though not especially
owy, they give a golden glow to the arching clump.

Like its namesake, bamboo muhly expands its territory by
eeping rhizomes, but it's nowhere near as pushy. A native
the desert Southwest, it thrives in dry soils, although it will
ow taller with more moisture. Plant it wherever you want
give a lush look to a dry garden, or where you need a

graceful, filmy accent. It also takes well to large pots, whe
it can spill over the sides.

How to Grow

Sun. Well-drained ordinary soil. Also does well in dry a
rocky or sandy soil. Sulks in heavy clay; lighten those so
with plenty of sand or grow in pots instead. Excelle
drought tolerance. Propagate by dividing the scaly rhizom

■ *filipes*
Purple muhly
Zones 7–9. P/Cl/W
Height: 18–24 in. Spread: 12–18 in.

Ethereal in flower, this grass produces gauzy clouds sim
lar in effect to purple love grass, though taller. The flowe
create a filmy mass 2–4 ft. above the foliage, in mid- to la
fall. It's a wonder to watch the panicle of flowers emerge a
change from its narrow, dark purple beginnings to its fir
cloud of glory. The rest of the season, purple muhly is a qui
clump of tufted leaves. This American native comes fro
moist pine barrens along the Gulf and southeastern Atlant
coasts. It's showy in masses. Slip a few plants into a bord
for late-season splendor, or try it with a background of ne
dled or broad-leaved evergreens.

How to Grow

Sun to light shade. Moist, well-drained soil. Does especial
well in moist sand and in rocky, light soils. Grows well in ga
dens near the coast.

■ *pubescens* *p. 160*
Soft blue Mexican muhly
Zones 9–10. P/Cl/C
Height: 8–12 in. Spread: 8–12 in.

This is one of many perennial muhly grasses worth a t
in the garden. Although it lacks the flowering clouds of *M
filipes*, it does have a commendable neatly mounded hab
and lovely soft foliage. The moderately narrow $1/4$–$3/8$-in
wide leaves are an excellent blue-green color, and their dow
hairs catch every drop of dew for a bejeweled effect. As co
weather approaches, the foliage takes on a reddish tinge.
dies back in cold winters. The soft spikes of late-sprin
blooming flowers are held above the foliage. They are an a
pealing gray-blue with a hint of purple and look pretty in
small bouquet as well as in the garden. Plant in groups c
singly in a dry, naturalistic landscape, or combine it with sa
(*Salvia officinalis*), lavender, and other Mediterranean plan
of complementary colors and contrasting textures.

How to Grow

Sun to part shade. Well-drained, light soils, including sandy and rocky soil. Good plant for coastal gardens. May self-sow. Propagate by seed or division. Like other plants recently introduced to gardens, the full extent of the hardiness and tolerance of this grass is not yet known. Its native habitat is in mountain cliffs and canyons of Mexico; it may be cold-tolerant farther north than Zone 9.

rigens   *p. 161*

Deer grass

Zones 7–9. P/Cl/C

Height: 2–4 ft. Spread: 3 ft.

This cool-season perennial grass grows in dense clumps of slender, gray-green leaves. Unlike other cool-season types, it stays green right through summer, even in the driest gardens. The slim flower spikes are packed with tiny seeds and lack the hairlike awns that give the flowers of other muhlys a feathery softness. Try it in a naturalistic dry garden of lemon marigold, artemisias, and euphorbias, or as a ground cover on a slope for cool-looking cover in hot summer. Used for basket-making. In the San Francisco Bay area, it is grown as accent in industrial sites, especially the Hewlett-Packard facilities. Nice alternative to pampas grass in California.

How to Grow

Full sun to part shade. Widespread in its natural western range, it grows just about anywhere except in waterlogged soils. Does best in moist soil, but its deep roots can plumb underground water. Also tolerates alkaline and saline soils.

Oryzopsis

(Orysopsis)

or-ee-zop´sis

Gramineae. Grass family

Mostly perennial grasses of slender tufting habit and narrow or open panicles, depending on the species. The genus includes about 35 or so species from North America and Eurasia. The American species are mostly western natives; a few are native to the East and some more widespread. The botanical name comes from the Greek *oryza*, rice, and *opsis*, appearance, and alludes to the resemblance to true rice (*Oryza sativa*). The leaves and seeds make good forage for wild and ranch grazers, and the seeds were once an important food to Native Americans.

■ *hymenoides* *p. 161*
Indian rice grass, Indian millet, silkgrass
Zones 7–10. P/Cl/C
Height: 12–30 in. Spread: 12–24 in.

A beautiful airy grass with fine-textured foliage and vibrant, delicate open panicles of small seeds. The inflorescences are intriguing at close range: the silky-tufted seeds are held on thin wiry stems that kink and curve. In the wild, it was once common from Mexico through Texas and the desert West, as well as in the Canadian plains from Manitoba to British Columbia. Like many native plants, it has been decimated by grazing, development, and replacement by invasive alien species.

A cool-season perennial, it's at its best in spring; by early summer it is dormant tan, although the clump remains standing into winter. In a low-water garden, where plants go dormant in hot summer, it looks like a natural part of the cycle. Plant with flowering drought-tolerant perennials and silver-foliaged plants. It's a great grass for fresh or dried arrangements.

How to Grow
Sun. Flourishes in dry soils akin to those of its natural desert and plains habitat. Also grows in ordinary, very well drained garden soil. Adapted to extremely dry desert conditions, it fails to thrive if given too much water in summer. Propagate by seed. May self-sow. Limits of cold tolerance are yet to be established; it may grow in colder regions than Zone 7.

anicum

an´ih-kum

raminaee. Grass family

A diverse genus of annual and perennial species, between 00 and 600 worldwide. Many are North American natives, cluding the excellent ornamental switch grass *(P. virgatum),* ne of the dominant species of the tallgrass prairie that once lanketed the middle of the continent. The common name of e genus, panic grass, is derived from *Panicum,* a Latin name r millet. (*Panicum miliaceum* is white proso millet, a com-on ingredient in birdseed mixes.)

Panic grasses generally grow in a luxuriant clump of long aves and have gloriously light and airy panicles of flowers. plethora of new cultivars, and others that were developed grass-appreciating Germany, are becoming available to merican gardeners. Translations of the German cultivar ames are included in the descriptions below; plants may be sted in catalogs and references in either or both languages.

clandestinum

eer tongue grass

ones 4–9. P/Cl/W

leight: 1–4 ft. Spread: 2–3 ft.

At first glance, this warm-season grass looks nothing like *Panicum.* Its leaves are short and wide and stick out from e stem at sharp angles every few inches like a bamboo. /hen it blooms, though, you can see the family resemblance. he flowers are pretty panicles at the tip of each stem, and e airy seed heads last for months. The slightly furry stems f this grass are reddish brown and contrast beautifully with e bright green, inch-wide leaves. In the wild, deer tongue rass grows in woods and at wood's edge. Its stems may grow rect or stretch laxly along the ground, especially after looming. Leaves begin to emerge in early spring, and the esh, light green foliage is appealing with spring ephemeral ildflowers or with bulbs. It's also a beautiful contrast to lacy r leathery ferns, and it looks as good as a small bamboo long streams and water. Plant in masses in a shade or wood-nd garden or edge paths to create a wide swathe of beauti-l yellow fall color.

low to Grow

art sun to moderate shade. Leaves are deeper green in shade; ey tend to look sickly yellowish in full sun. Moist, humusy il is best, but it will also grow well in heavier soils. Does ell in humid, hot summers. Support the clump with a loop f wire to keep it erect when flowering. It dies back in win-r and needs no cutting back.

■ *virgatum* *p. 162*
Switch grass
Zones 5–9. P/Cl/W
Height: 3–7 ft. Spread: 2–3 ft.

Spectacular in flower, this perennial grass grows in narrow erect clumps. Some plants may have leaves with a decided curl, while others are rigidly erect. Either way, the cloud of flowers creates an eye-catching contrast atop the vertical column of foliage. The slender leaves, 1–2 ft. long, are medium green in summer, turning bright yellow, gold, or orange in fall. Flower panicles open dark reddish purple to silvery white in midsummer, forming an airy mass 12–16 in. above the foliage that mellows to beige in fall.

This North American native is well adapted to the vagaries of our climate and tolerates both wet and dry sites. A mass planting is a sight to remember. The sturdy clumps can screen undesirable views or define intimate spaces. They also add rich, long-lasting fall color and winter interest to perennial borders. The unimproved species is an excellent garden plant; the named cultivars listed below are superb. All are good in Zones 5–9 unless otherwise noted and can be grown as described below.

How to Grow
Full or part sun. Ordinary or unimproved soil. Cut down to the ground in early spring. May spread, but is easily controlled. May self-sow. Propagate established clumps by division. Thrives in coastal conditions.

'Cloud Nine' is a medium-tall cultivar (4–6 ft.) with gray green foliage that makes a beautiful foil for yellow coneflowers (*Ratibida* species), yellow-flowered cup plant *(Silphium perfoliatum)*, and other silphiums. Or plant a meadow patch with annual sunflowers, especially the branching types (See photo on p. 162.)

'Haense Herms', sometimes called red switch grass, comes into its own in fall, with intense orange-red foliage in early to midautumn, deepening to plum purple as the season progresses. Its abundant flowers are also suffused with red tones. This grass has a looser, more weeping habit than other cultivars, growing as wide (3–4 ft.) as it is tall. (See photo on p. 163.)

'Heavy Metal' grows in a straight stunning column (3–5 ft.) of metallic blue foliage that contrasts wonderfully in the border with the colors and softer shapes of most perennials and annuals. Its good yellow fall color is almost a bonus. Like other switch grasses, this one maintains its form in the winter er garden, when the stiff leaves bleach to tan. Try a clump or three with a drift of pink beebalm (*Monarda* spp.) and a sprawling mat of soft pink primrose *(Oenothera speciosa).* Or go for bold and plant 'Heavy Metal' with other shouters like hot orange nasturtiums and orange-red Mexican sunflower *(Tithonia rotundifolia).* Zones 4–9. (See photo on p. 163.) Another good cultivar with stiffly upright form is tall switch-grass, *P. virgatum* 'Strictum'.

Rotstrahlbusch' ('Red Rays') tops many lists as the best red cultivar. It grows to 4 ft., and the foliage intensifies to a burnished red in midsummer to early autumn. Send shock waves through your garden by combining it with strong pink fall asters, or cool things off by planting with a foamy bed of blue mistflower *(Eupatorium coelestinum).* (See photo on p. 164.)

'Squaw' is a 3–4 ft. clump like a fountain spilling from the center in all directions, turning purple-red by late summer. (See photo on p. 164.) 'Warrior' has a similar punch. Both cultivars are gorgeous with the bright orange, red, and yellow fall foliage of deciduous trees and shrubs. The silvery plumes of early-blooming miscanthus cultivars, such as 'Flamingo', also make a strong partner, or try planting with cool-season grasses such as *Koeleria* — their tan dormant foliage will play up the deep tones of the red switch grasses. Another red-leaved cultivar, *P. virgatum* 'Rehbraun' ('Red-Brown'), has a muddier hue.

Pennisetum

pen-nih-see´tum
Gramineae. Grass family

Annual or perennial grasses with flat leaves and narrow, dense, fuzzy flower spikes that spray outward, giving the genus the common name "fountain grass." All are ornamental in mixed beds, rock gardens, and with other grasses, and they thrive in containers. The flowers are also pretty in arrangements.

About 80 species, most native to tropical or warm climates. Some grasses in this genus, generally the wider-leaved, late-blooming cultivars, such as 'Moundry' and 'National Arboretum', have become pesky weeds in parts of the country, especially California. If you live in a mild climate, check with your county extension office or the closest branch of the Nature Conservancy for advice on fountain grasses to avoid. Many experts are recommending Californians pass on the genus altogether.

■ *alopecuroides (see below for photos)*
(P. japonicum)
Fountain grass, Chinese pennisetum, Australian fountain grass
Zones 5–9. P/Cl/W
Height: 3–4 ft. Spread: 3–4 ft.

This warm-season perennial grass offers three-season interest. It makes a vibrant, flowing fountain of fine-textured leaves, dark green in summer and warm apricot, almond, or orange in fall, gradually bleaching to pale tan. It flowers freely from midsummer to midfall, with stems of fluffy foxtaillike spikes spilling outward like a fountain. Flowers may shade from reddish purple to coppery tan. An excellent plant to combine with spring bulbs — its fresh spring growth complements the bulb flowers, and it soon grows to cover the yellowing bulb leaves. It's also good as a ground cover or transitional plant bridging natural and more formal areas. The lovely arching form is mirrored in ponds and has a softening effect on rock or paving. A number of cultivars are on the market, including three diminutive fountain grasses.

'Cassian' is a free-flowering cultivar with outstanding fall color — it turns a rich golden yellow. The plant is dwarf, but the flowering stems can reach 2 ft. long, creating a luxuriant spray of soft spikes. Put it near the front of the border for close-up admiration. (See photo on p. 165.)

'Hameln' is another downsized version. It has very fine foliage and shorter flowering spikes and flower heads that are just the right fit for the mixed border. It blooms in early to midsummer. Zones 4–9.

The most diminutive of the small-scale cultivars, 'Little Bunny' grows in a petite tuft of leaves (6–12 in. round) and carries short, fluffy flower heads. Good for rock gardens or on a slope with soapwort and other mat-forming or small perennials. The little flowers are charming in fresh and dried arrangements. Zones 6–8.

A magnified version of the species, 'Japonicum' is the largest fountain grass cultivar, at 4–5 ft. tall and 4 ft. wide and bearing huge panicles of misty flowers. It is beautiful near water. Fine yellow fall color. Zones 6–8.

Two unusual fountain grasses, black-flowering 'Moudry' (see photo on p. 165) and the improved version, 'National Arboretum', are invasive grasses in warm climates. They seed themselves with a free hand and can escape from the garden into the lawn or the surrounding wild landscape. To lessen the risk of self-sowing, clip off flower spikes after enjoying them for a few weeks in the garden. They bloom later than other fountain grasses, in late summer to early fall. The spikes are dark, glistening brown when they emerge, and fluff out into reddish purple at the tips, with darker hearts, as they mature. Flowering is inconsistent. Some years, the flowers are held well out from the foliage; other times, they may be hidden among the leaves. 'National Arboretum' puts on a good show every year.

How to Grow

Full sun in the North; part shade in hotter climates. Does best in moist, well-drained soil, but tolerates other sites, too. Grows in acidic or alkaline soils. Tolerates dry spells, but the leaves get pale and curl up. Cut back old foliage in early spring, especially if planted with bulbs. Can be (but doesn't need to be) divided every five to six years. The center of the clump may die out, but that gap is noticeable only in early spring and doesn't matter later. Voles and mice may feed on the crown in winter. May be inexplicably short-lived, lasting only a few years in the garden. May self-sow. Grow from seed or propagate by division.

■ *macrostachyum* 'Burgundy Giant'   *p. 166*
Zones 9–10. P/Cl/W
Height: 4–5 ft. Spread: 4–5 ft.

A tropical grass from southern India with wider leaves and a less fountainlike habit than *P. alopecuroides*. Only the cultivar 'Burgundy Giant', a red-leaved plant, is commonly grown. Although it is very tender and will be killed at the first touch of freezing temperatures, it's so fast-growing that you can enjoy it as an annual in cold-winter climates. It has wide, strappy leaves up to an inch across and stout, upright stems. In midsummer long flower spikes, up to a foot long, arch above the wide column of foliage on erect stems, nodding like the foxtail grasses along roadsides.

The rich maroon foliage of this grass invites combination with many other grasses, shrubs, and perennials. Hot red, orange-red, and yellow flowers like dahlias, Klondike cosmos, black-eyed Susans, and daylilies create a dramatic effect. Try it with pale pink and white flowers like nicotiana, geraniums, cosmos, and petunias, for subtle beauty. Leaves and flowers are outstanding in fresh arrangements.

How to Grow
Sun. Moist but well-drained soil. The flags of leaves will rip and shred in strong winds; plant it in a protected site. Water regularly if rain is scarce. Cut back in early spring. Propagate by division. You can also try propagating by stem cutting rooted in sand and planted out the following spring.

■ *orientale* *p. 166*
Oriental fountain grass
Zones 7–9. P/Cl/W
Height: 1–2 ft. Spread: 1–2 ft.
This beautiful perennial grass forms gray-green clumps of arching foliage topped with equally arching spikes of pinkish-purple flowers. It starts flowering two to three weeks earlier than *P. alopecuroides,* in midspring in mild-winter climates and late spring to early summer in northern climates, where it is grown as an annual. The flowers last a long time, finally disintegrating by fall. Like other fountain grasses, the foliage mellows to golden tan and lasts all winter.

How to Grow
Sun to part or light shade. Well-drained soil. Thrives in sandy soils. Lighten heavy clay soils with generous helpings of compost, leaf mold, or aged manure. May self-sow. Propagate by seed or division.

■ *setaceum*
Tender fountain grass, crimson fountain grass
Zones 8–9. P/Cl/W
Height: 2–3 ft. Spread: 2–3 ft.
Tender perennial grown as an annual north of Zone 8. Makes an arching or mounded clump of fine-textured rusty-green foliage. The fluffy, nodding spikes of rose or purple flowers, which can reach 12 in. long, are held well above the foliage from June through fall. Effective as a specimen or massed. Nice with pink-flowering nicotiana, which accents the pink tints of the grass flowers. This species self-sows and has become a weed in warm areas, such as California, where it is listed as one of the invasive exotics most difficult to control. The species *Pennisetum clandestinum,* Kikuyu grass, is also classified as a noxious weed there.

How to Grow

Full or part sun. Ordinary or unimproved soil. Somewhat drought-tolerant. When grown as an annual, it may need staking, especially in windy areas. As a perennial, cut foliage down in fall or spring. Self-sows and can be a weedy pest.

setaceum 'Rubrum' *p. 167*
(*P. setaceum* 'Atropurpureum'; also 'Purpureum', 'Atrosanguineum', and 'Cupreum')
Tender purple fountain grass, crimson fountain grass
Zones 9–10. P/Cl/W
Height: 3–4 ft. Spread: 2–3 ft.

This tender cultivar can be enjoyed as an annual in colder climates thanks to its fast growth and long season of flowering. The eye-catching burgundy foliage makes a good contrast in flower beds and is striking in large containers. It also makes a stunning mass planting, especially if silver-leaved artemisias are planted in front to emphasize the deep color of the grass. The long, arching flowers, which can be up to a foot long, are purple-red when they emerge, then mature to softer reddish purple and finally to brownish tan. The plant turns soft tan with a freeze.

'Rubrum Dwarf' is a downsized version, under 2 ft. tall, an excellent size for perennial gardens and containers. The foliage is ruddy and the arching flowers have a rich crimson hue. Try it in front of climbing pink roses like 'New Dawn', or old shrub roses like 'Koenigin von Danemark', where its fountain of leaves will mirror the arching form of the rose and its deep color will make the pale roses glow.

How to Grow

Sun. Well-drained soil; will thrive in clay and sandy, rocky, or loam soils. Good for coastal gardens. Propagate by division.

villosum *p. 167*
(*P. longistylum*)
Feathertop, tender white-flowered fountain grass
Zones 8–9. P/Cl/W
Height: 24–30 in. Spread: 18–24 in.

Valued for fluffy white plumes that look like elongated bunny tails, this tender perennial grass can be grown as an annual in cold-winter climates. It blooms from July through September. Best combined with flowering annuals or perennials that can cover the irregular mound of foliage — which isn't particularly attractive — and help support the flower stalks during rains or stormy weather. It's also an attention-getter when combined with dark-flowered 'Moudry' fountain grass.

How to Grow

Full or part sun. Ordinary soil; also thrives in sand. Propa
gate by seed. Good for coastal gardens. Not seriously weed
but it has escaped in areas from Michigan to Texas. Doesn
last into winter; cut to the ground in fall.

Phalaris

fa-lay´ris

Gramineae. Grass family

Annual or perennial grasses, most with spreading rhizome
and thick, densely packed, pointed inflorescences. About 1
species from the north temperate zone, some of which ar
used as food for cage birds, as cotton sizing, and hay for live
stock.

■ *arundinacea* 'Picta' *p. 168*
(*P. arundinacea* var. *picta*)
Ribbon grass, gardener's garters
Zones 4–9. P/R/W
Height: 2–4 ft. Spread: 2–4 ft. or more

One of the first grasses grown as an ornamental, this plar
is noted for its variegated foliage and fortitude. The uprigh
stems hold green-and-white-striped leaves 4–10 in. long. On
clump can lighten a dark-colored corner or provide a foil fo
clashing colors in a perennial border. The pinkish whit
flowers in midsummer are not particularly ornamental.

In all but very dry desert gardens, ribbon grass is a ram
pant grower, spreading by creeping roots. Choose a plantin
site carefully: once it's established, eradication is difficult be
cause the grass springs up from any pieces of root left in th
soil. You can control its spread by planting in a bottomles
container or in defined areas such as parking lot islands.
makes a tough ground cover and the rhizomes are an effec
tive soil stabilizer. It can also be grown as an aquatic, plante
in shallow water a few inches deep or in a container sur
rounded by deep water.

'Dwarf Garters' is a more manageable cultivar. This short
(12–15 in. tall) spreads more slowly than its taller relative
but in the border you may want to confine it with barrier
for peace of mind. It does best in part to light shade, not i
sun.

'Feesey', also sold as 'Feasey's Form', is a fine-textured cul
tivar suffused with pink, especially in spring. The whitis
flowers are showier than those of old-fashioned ribbon gras
but the plant spreads as aggressively. Best used in masses o

ong water. To emphasize the pink tints of the fresh foliage, ant with spring-blooming perennials in soft pink shades, ch as hardy geraniums, soapwort, and rockcress. 'Feesey' lerates some shade; grow in part shade in hot summer clintes. (See photo on p. 168.)

ow to Grow

all or part sun. Not fussy about soil: tolerates sand or clay, idic or alkaline conditions, wet or dry sites, some sea salt, ad standing water. In most areas, the foliage is pretty in ring and early summer but turns brown by late summer. at it back to 6 in. and it will sprout fresh new growth. Eas- propagated by division.

hormium

r'mee-um

gavaceae. Agave family

Large clumping plants with spearlike leaves. Fibers from e leaves are woven into fishing nets and fabrics. Only two ecies, native to New Zealand.

tenax p. 169

ew Zealand flax

ones 8–10. P/Cl

eight: 8–9 ft. Spread: 8–9 ft.

This plant has the same architectural effect as a hefty grass. he sword-shaped leaves, up to 9 ft. long and 5 in. wide, ow in crowded clumps of irislike fans. Clusters of reddish own trumpet-shaped flowers are borne on tall naked stalks summer. Compact 3–5-ft. cultivars fit into smaller gardens ad make bold punctuation marks in a flower border. Many ultivars are named for their gorgeous leaf color: purple-red tropurpureum', deep purple-red 'Rubrum', or 'Bronze'. riegated cultivars 'Maori Sunset', 'Maori Queen', and 'Sunowner', all have bronze leaves striped with red, pink, and eamy white. 'Yellow Wave' has cheerful yellow-striped een leaves.

ow to Grow

all or part sun. Ordinary, well-drained soil. Plant from coniners and allow plenty of space — phormiums get big fast. eeds no care beyond the removal of dead or damaged leaves ad old flower stalks. May freeze back in cold winters, but covers in one season. Can be divided, but you'll need several helpers to tackle a large specimen.

Phyllostachys

fil-lo-stak´is

Gramineae. Grass family

A large and useful group of hardy bamboos. Some gro quite tall, and all spread to make thickets or groves. Th young shoots are eaten as a vegetable, and mature culm (stems) are used for fishing rods, plant stakes, fences, and tir ber. About 60 species, native to China.

■ *aureosulcata* *p. 169*

Yellow groove bamboo

Zones 6–10. P/R

Height: 15–20 ft. Spread: 15–20 ft. or more

One of the hardiest running (grove-making) bamboos. Th woody, upright culms are rich green with yellow grooves th run vertically from node to node. They grow up to $1\frac{1}{2}$ i thick and are good for plant stakes and light fencing. Th narrow lance-shaped leaves are papery thin and light gree If spread is curbed, these bamboos can be used as a screen hedge.

How to Grow

Full or part sun. Ordinary soil and watering. Plant divisio in spring, container-grown plants anytime. Zone 5 gardene can grow these species like herbaceous perennials. The culm may freeze to the ground, but the roots are hardy to –20°F protected with a layer of snow or mulch. These bamboo spread by underground rhizomes and can send up new shoo 20–30 ft. into your neighbor's yard. Mowing the shoots wi a lawnmower won't keep the plant from spreading. You nee to dig a trench and install a concrete, metal, fiberglass, c heavy plastic curb 18–24 in. deep when you first plant th bamboo. Don't be fooled into thinking cold winters will kee the plants under control; new shoots will surface in spring f from the parent. Maintenance is simple. Remove the oldes tattered culms at ground level. Thin culms to create a grov Shear hedges as desired.

■ *nigra* *p. 170*

Black bamboo

Zones 7–10. P/R

Height: 10–25 ft. Spread: 15–25 ft. or more

This bamboo has shiny black culms up to 1 in. thick ar narrow, dark green leaves. It strikes a deep note again brighter green foliage, and like other bamboos, adds grace masonry walls or fences. A confined grove is lovely in Japanese-style garden. If you don't want to let it run in you garden, plant it in a generous container; put the container c our patio or wherever the smooth black stems can be admired at close range. Also grown as a houseplant.

How to Grow
Same as *P. aureosulcata*.

Poa
poe´uh
Gramineae. Grass family
This large genus includes many familiar lawn grasses, such as Kentucky blue grass. More than 250 species (some authorities say 500 species) of annuals and perennials are native to North America, Eurasia, and other temperate regions of the world. In America, they are valuable forage and pasture grasses. Grass enthusiasts have introduced a few species to the horticultural trade.

compressa
Australian blue grass
Zones 8–10. P/Cl/C
Height: 1–2 ft. Spread: 1–2 ft.
This cool-season perennial holds promise as an ornamental grass for warm climates. It grows in dense clumps that green up early, making it a good choice for covering a slope. Despite its name, it doesn't look blue. Rolled leaf blades hide the blue undersides but give the grass its fine texture. The flowers are airy panicles that quiver in the breeze and ripen to golden tan.

How to Grow

Sun. Widely adaptable to soil types, but does best in mois
well-drained soils. Drought-tolerant. Good for coastal cond
tions. Like other recently introduced grasses, the limits of th
one aren't fully known. It may prove to be more cold-hard
and is worth the experiment if you need a tough, adaptabl
grass.

Rhynchelytrum

(Rhychelytrum)
rink-ee-ly´trum
Gramineae. Grass family

Native to Africa, the natal grasses get their botanical nam
from their peculiar seeds: *rhynch* is Greek for beak; *elytrum*
scale. They are annuals and perennials with showy, fluffy par
icles of flowers. Taxonomists disagree on how many grasse
belong to the genus; some say as few as 14, while others a
sign about 40 to this group.

■ *repens* *p. 170*
(Tricholaena rosea; Tricholaena repens)
Natal grass, ruby grass
Zones 9–10. P/W
Height: 1–4 ft., usually about 1–2 ft. Spread: 1–2 ft.

Natal grass is a short-lived perennial that creates a billow
cloud of soft pink flowers. Its showy flowers and long bloor
time — from summer almost through fall — make it im
mensely decorative in the garden, but it is a rampant self
sower in warm areas and has become a pest in Florida. Th
name ruby grass comes from the color of the newly emerge
flowers, which are tinged purple to pink-red. As they mature
they soften to pinkish or creamy tan. The soft flowers are a
excellent contrast to the dramatic spikes of bronze or varie
gated New Zealand flax *(Phormium tenax)* either together i
large containers or in the garden. Or you can back them wit
the dark foliage of purple smoke bush. The flowers are beau
tiful in fresh arrangements. Natal grass can be grown as a
annual in cold climates. Neither running nor clumping, nata
grass grows in single stalks like wheat.

How to Grow

Sun. Will grow in almost all soils, but needs good drainage
Good for coastal gardens. Self-sows. Easy to grow from seed
or propagate by division.

accharum

ah-kar´um

Gramineae family

Large, robust perennial grasses of the tropical Old World, his genus includes more than 12 species (as many as 37 if grasses classified as *Erianthus* are counted). The hard stems are jointed like cane or bamboo, and the leaf blades are wide, arching, and often tipped with dangerously sharp points. Sugarcane *(S. officinarum)*, which is sometimes grown as an ornamental, is a member of the genus. If you've ever bought a piece of the sweet stalk at the grocery store, you'll have an idea of the thickness of this plant's stout, jointed stems. Cultivars of sugarcane are being developed for their ornamental possibilities in warm gardens. Growers are selecting for various combinations of color in both cane and leaves.

officinarum 'Pele's Smoke'

ed sugarcane

Zones 9–10. P/Cl/W

Height: 10–15 ft. Spread: 10–12 ft.

This huge grass has striking foliage in rich deep maroon-purple that looks almost purple-black in some lights. It grows in an upright clump, arching near the top. The stems are thick and jointed, up to 3 in. in diameter, and are just as richly colored as the foliage. The leaves are wide and strappy with rough edges. Flowers are a rarity. Plant as a specimen or in a grouping with other grasses. It makes a good background plant for grasses with light-colored flowers, such as 'Flamingo' miscanthus.

How to Grow

Sun. Thrives in many soils, but needs moisture and good drainage. Grows incredibly fast; worth trying as an annual in colder climates. Be careful working around this plant; the leaf blades are sharp and have pointed tips. Propagate by rooting cuttings of mature canes in moist sand, or hack a piece off an established clump.

Sasa

sa´suh

Gramineae. Grass family

Low-growing, spreading bamboos with broad leaves. They rarely flower. About 25 species, native to eastern Asia.

■ *palmata*
(*S. paniculata; S. senanensis*)
Running bamboo
Zones 7–10. P/R
Height: 6 ft. or more. Spread: 6 ft. or more

A rampantly spreading bamboo with slender erect stem. Papery thin, bright green leaves are clustered at the tips of the stems and branches; they keep their good green color even in winter. Stems are often streaked with purple, an interesting effect up close. Underground runners spread fast. Use it to control erosion on hillsides or streambanks, or install 18-in. deep barriers at planting time and use it for a quick tropical or Oriental effect.

How to Grow
Sun or shade. Spreads fast in rich, moist soil; not quite so fast in ordinary conditions, but don't be lulled into thinking you can control it. Curb with a deep metal, fiberglass, or concrete barrier at planting time. Propagate by division. Dig up sections of 5–6 stems in early spring. Try to keep soil around the roots, and replant quickly. Needs little care — just cut old or shabby stems to the ground in spring. Doesn't tolerate desert heat or drought. Worth a try in Zone 6. It may freeze to the ground but will recover.

■ *veitchii* *p. 171*
(*S. albomarginata*)
Running bamboo, silver-edge bamboo, kuma zasa
Zones 7–10. P/R
Height: 2–3 ft. Spread: 3 ft. or more

A striking ground cover for shade, with broad, papery bright green leaves that turn creamy white around the edges

fall. The variegated effect lasts all winter. Leaves are clustered at the ends of the slender canes. Indispensable for
Japanese gardens; use with liriope, azaleas, water-smoothed
stones, and bamboo fences.

How to Grow

Like *S. palmata*.

Schizachyrium

sky-zack´ree-um

Gramineae. Grass family

Mostly perennial grasses with a bunching habit. Closely related to Andropogon. More than 90 species, mostly tropical.

scoparium *p. 171*
(*Andropogon scoparius*)
Little bluestem
Zones 3–9. P/Cl/W
Height: 2–3 ft. Spread: 12–18 in.

A perennial warm-season native of the American tallgrass
prairie, little bluestem is neither little nor blue. It forms erect
clumps reaching knee-high or better (some plants may top 5
ft.) with slender green leaves that have a hint of blue near the
base.

It's in the fall that this grass really shines, maturing to a
burnished orange that is magnificent with the fall foliage of
trees and shrubs. The color intensifies when the grass is wet
after a rain. The summer flowers mature into fluffy seed

heads that persist into winter. Borne along flexible stems tha
stand up even in a heavy snowfall, the small clusters of see
heads sparkle when backlit by the slanting rays of the sun. I
the wintry landscape of bare dark branches, and especiall
against snow, this grass is unwavering as a flame.

Broomsedge *(Andropogon virginicus)*, often confused wit
little bluestem, has leafier stems, especially near the top, an
less showy flowers: the small tufts are snuggled inside th
bracts of the leafy stem instead of curling outward and down
ward like those of *Schizachyrium scoparius*. To make matter
more confusing, it often hybridizes with little bluestem
Learning to tell the difference was once critical to land buy
ers because the presence of little bluestem indicated fertile so
good for growing wheat, while a lot of broomsedge mean
that the land was overgrazed and the soil lean. In the land
scape, though, broomsedge is just as appealing as littl
bluestem, with the same orange fall and winter color.

Little bluestem is an outstanding grass for the mixed bor
der, where it mingles well with fall-blooming perennials suc
as short cultivars of purple New England asters. Its neat gree
tufts provide good structure in the summer garden, too. It ca
be used as a large-scale ground cover on dry sites, for erosio
control, or as a transition between tended and natural areas
The seeds will attract native sparrows and other small birds
The fall foliage cut in bunches adds color and softness t
dried arrangements of seeds and pods, or it can be twisted o
braided into wreaths.

'The Blues', a bit taller than the species (up to 4 ft.), ha
gorgeous gray-blue foliage in tightly erect clumps that pro
vide excellent vertical line in the garden. It is beautiful wit
pink astilbe, blue Russian sage, or other soft-textured peren
nials. Zones 4–9. The more compact cultivar, 'Blaze' (1–3 ft
high and 2–3 ft. wide), was selected for its excellent fall an
winter color, which ranges from purplish orange to russet o
reddish purple. It is commonly planted along highways in th
Midwest and used to reclaim old strip mines in coal-minin
areas.

How to Grow

Full or part sun. Ordinary or unimproved soil. Flourishes i
hot weather, humidity, and dry soil. Thrives in sandy soil a
well as clay. Shrugs off drought. Can self-sow, but usuall
doesn't. Propagate by dividing older clumps. When sowin
large areas, use a water-filled lawn roller to push seeds we
into soil. Cut back once a year, in early spring.

Schoenplectus

show-en-plek´tus

Cyperaceae. Sedge family

Annual or perennial grasslike plants that usually spread by creeping rhizomes. Stems may have the typical "edges" of the sedge family, three-angled to the touch, or they may be cylindrical. The stems form the "foliage" of these plants; true leaves are often absent altogether. About 80 species, found on almost every continent.

■ *lacustris* ssp. *tabernaemontani* 'Zebrinus'

S. *tabernaemontana* 'Zebrinus'; *Scirpus lacustris* ssp. (or var.) *tabernaemontana* 'Zebrinus')

Zebra rush, banded bulrush

Zones 4–9. P/R

Height: 2–4 ft. Spread: 4 ft. or more

The erect, cylindrical "leaves" of zebra rush are spangled with horizontal yellow bands that look as if they've been splashed by dappled sunlight. Brownish flowers appear atop the speckled stems in summer and hang on into fall and winter, when the rush turns first yellow, then brown.

This bog plant is a good edge plant for ponds, where it will spread into the shallows, creating a graceful transition between land and water. Its porcupine-like foliage is a great contrast to the broad leaves and golden flowers of the western skunk cabbage *(Lysichiton americanus)*, a striking plant well known as an ornamental in Britain but not in its native America. Zebra rush also looks good with a spread of buttery yellow marsh marigolds *(Caltha palustris)* beside it.

How to Grow

Sun. Moist or wet soil or shallow water, to 1 ft. deep. Transplant young plants into the bog garden or at the pond edge in spring. Allow them room to spread, which they'll do at a moderately fast pace. Propagate by division, separating the rhizomes in spring.

Scirpus

skir´pus

Cyperaceae. Sedge family

Perennial grasslike plants that spread from rhizomatous roots. The erect stems are leafy, and flowers are borne in loose clusters at the top. About 100 species from around the world.

■ *cernuus*
(Scirpus filiformis; Isolepsis gracilis; Isolepsis cernua)
Low bulrush
Zones 8–10. P/Cl
Height: 6–12 in. Spread: 12–18 in.

The thin, hairlike stems and leaves of this interesting rush grow in a hummocky clump that looks like a mop-top Beatles wig. Tiny whitish conelike flowers dot the mound of foliage like a handful of fireflies or light-carrying fiber optics. (It is sometimes listed as "fiber optics grass.") Low bulrush is evergreen in Zone 10 and some parts of Zone 9; cut it back in other zones once foliage has gone dormant after frost. Plant this moisture-lover along the rocky edge of a garden pool, where it can spill prettily over the rocks.

How to Grow
Sun to light or part shade; if plant yellows, move to a shadier site. Moist to wet soil or very shallow water. Will also adapt to life in a container if you keep it well watered. Transplant a young plant to the garden in spring. Propagate by division in spring.

Semiarundinaria
sem-ee-uh-run-di-nay´ree-uh
Gramineae. Grass family

Running bamboos with woody culms that form tall, open thickets. They rarely flower. About 20 species, native to eastern Asia.

■ *murielae*   p. 172
Running bamboo
Zones 7–10. P/R
Height: 10–15 ft. Spread: 10 ft. or more

This bamboo makes a tall, slow-spreading clump and isn't too invasive. Slender arching culms create a weeping-willow effect, but with denser foliage that makes a good screen.

How to Grow
Sun to moderate shade. Grows and spreads very slowly in unimproved soil. Gets taller and lusher in fertile soil amended with organic matter. Divide in very early spring, taking clumps of 3–5 stems with a good root ball, and replant promptly. Remove old or damaged stems. Trouble-free.

Sesleria

ez-lair´ee-uh
Gramineae. Grass family
   More than 20 species of mostly perennial, usually small grasses. Native to the moors and chalk highlands of Europe, they are often called moor grasses.

autumnalis   p. 172
Autumn moor grass
Zones 5–9. P/Cl/C
Height: 18 in. Spread: 18 in.
   Moor grasses aren't particularly ornamental, but they are undemanding and they offer evergreen foliage even in colder climates. This species has perky yellow-green color that brightens the shade under shrubs and trees, where you can plant it in low-maintenance sweeps. Narrow spikes of flowers push up in fall or in late spring in mild-winter areas.

How to Grow
Sun to light or part shade. Adapts to almost any soil. Tolerates drought. Thrives in coastal gardens and other difficult sites. Propagate by dividing in spring.

caerulea
Blue moor grass
Zones 5–9. P/Cl/C
Height: 6–12 in. Spread: 6–12 in.
   This perennial cool-season grass grows in a loose tussock of lax narrow foliage. A silvery gray glint on one side of the leaves gives the plant a bluish cast. The small spikes of flowers are greenish at first and mature to pale whitish tan. *S. albicans,* also called blue moor grass, is a very similar, somewhat taller species with striking mauve flowers; the two species are often confused.

How to Grow
Sun to part or light shade; plant in part or light shade in hot-summer climates. Moisture-retentive soil. Propagate by division in spring or fall.

heufleriana   p. 173
Green moor grass
Zones 5–9. P/Cl/C
Height: 12–18 in. Spread: 12–18 in.
   The young leaves of this cool-season perennial grass are powdered with white, giving the tuft a cool, frosty look. An-

other tough moor grass, this one is good in difficult conditions as well as in the sharp drainage of a rock garden.

How to Grow
Sun to part or light shade; part or light shade in hot-summer
areas. Drought-tolerant, but stays greener with more moisture. Propagate by division in spring or fall.

Sorghastrum

sor-gas´trum
Gramineae. Grass family
   Perennial grasses with narrow leaves, important chiefly as
fodder. More than 13 species, mostly from tropical regions of
Africa and the Americas.

■ *nutans* p. 173
(S. avenaceum; Chrysopogon nutans)
Indian grass
Zones 4–9. P/Cl/W
Height: 3–8 ft., usually 3–5 ft. Spread: 2 ft.
   Native to the tallgrass prairie, Indian grass forms tall narrow clumps that make a good vertical accent in the border
or massed as a background or screen. The slender leaves are
light green or blue in summer, bronze or burnt orange in fall,
and rich gold in winter. Slender downy flower heads are con-
spicuous for several weeks in late summer or fall. They open
golden and darken to bronze and can be used in fresh or
dried arrangements. A graceful grass that combines beautifully with Maximilian sunflower, purple coneflower, and
other native prairie flowers.

The abundantly flowering cultivar 'Holt' was developed with an eye toward practicality — as an improved forage grass for cattle — but it is beautiful in the garden or meadow. Planted in mass behind a similar mass of mid-height deep purple fall asters *(Aster novae-angliae)* it makes a stunning autumn combination.

How to Grow

Full or part sun. Can get floppy if the soil is too rich and moist, but stands up well if grown in lean, dry soil. Tolerates heat but appreciates an occasional watering during long dry spells. Propagate by seed or division. Cut back once a year, in spring. May self-sow, especially in undisturbed prairie or meadow plantings.

nutans 'Sioux Blue' *p. 174*
'Sioux Blue' Indian grass
Zones 4–9. P/Cl/W
Height: 3–5 ft. Spread: 2–3 ft.

This dramatic silvery blue cultivar stands very erect, providing an eye-catching vertical accent in a mass planting or as a specimen combined with red- or pink-flowered plants such as *Salvia coccinea*. It also makes an exclamation point next to sprawling gray-leaved plants like artemisias and helichrysum. Turns golden tan with orange highlights in fall.

How to Grow
Same as *S. nutans*.

Spartina
par-teen´uh
Gramineae. Grass family

Perennial grasses that spread by rhizomatous roots, this genus is known as cord grass because the strong leaves of some species were once used to make cordage. About 15 species, native to Europe, Africa, America, and some islands.

pectinata *p. 174*
Prairie cord grass
Zones 4–9. P/R/W
Height: 4–6 ft. Spread: 6 ft. or more

Once found in marshy areas and lowlands from the Midwest to the East, this warm-season running grass of the American prairies has narrow arching leaves, spilling over in a fountain of greenery that turns golden tan in fall and winter. It is a determined spreader, so give it plenty of room to roam,

and plant well away from passersby and children's play areas;
its dangerously sharp-edged leaves can slice a finger in an in
stant. With these precautions in mind, this grass is a lovely
choice to naturalize in a wet area or at water's edge. The nar
row, shining inflorescences are pretty in a vase, either fresh
or dried.

How to Grow
Sun to part shade. Moist or wet soil; will also grow in dry
soils and is much more restrained in height and spreading
habit there. Wear leather gloves and a sturdy long-sleeved
shirt or jacket when working around this plant. Cut back in
early spring, or simply let new foliage push up through old
in naturalized plantings. Propagate by division any time dur
ing the growing season; cut back foliage first to make it an
easier and safer job.

Spodiopogon
spoe-dee-oh-poe´gon
Gramineae. Grass family
   A small genus of about nine species, almost all perennial
Only one of these is commonly grown as an ornamental. Na
tive to both temperate and tropical regions of Asia.

■ *sibiricus p. 175*
(Muhlenbergia alpestris)
Frost grass
Zones 5–9. P/Cl/W
Height: 2–3 ft. Spread: 2–3 ft. or more
   This clumping, warm-season perennial grass is often grown
for its open panicles that bloom in late summer and fall, but
the foliage habit is just as ornamental. The leaves jut out hor
izontally from the stems, giving it a look more like bamboo
than grass. It spreads at a slow to moderate rate by rhi
zomatous roots.
   Whether you use it singly, in a group, or in masses, frost
grass carries plenty of weight in the garden, especially in fall
Its foliage becomes brown with streaks and tints of deep pur
plish red. Take advantage of its fall color by planting it with
late-season perennials such as asters and sedum 'Autumn
Joy', or situate it in front of mugo pine or other evergreen
to show off the airy flowers. The flowers and foliage are at
tention-getters in fresh arrangements, especially when com
bined with pale pink chrysanthemums.

How to Grow

Light or part shade; sun in cool climates. It will also grow in deeper shade, but stake to keep it erect. Plant in moist but well-drained soil. Does best with regular watering or rainfall. Foliage becomes tattered in winter; cut back to ground in late fall. Propagate by division or seed in spring.

Sporobolus

spo-ro´bo-lus
Gramineae. Grass family

Annual or perennial grasses, usually clump-forming and fine-textured. Ripe seeds drop out of their hulls, giving these grasses the common name dropseed. About 100 species, native to the Old and New Worlds.

heterolepsis p. 175
Prairie dropseed, northern dropseed
Zones 4–8. P/Cl/W
Height: 18–30 in. Spread: 18–24 in.

An excellent plant to start with if you are new to ornamental grasses. It forms an upright arching mound of fine, long leaves, emerald green in summer, turning gold with orange tints in fall. The color is stunning in winter. Panicles of small, delicate flowers are held 2–3 ft. above the foliage in late summer. The flowers have a unique fragrance — some compare it to buttered popcorn, others to coriander or melted wax. Pick them fresh for an intriguing touch in arrangements. Prairie dropseed can be grown as an accent plant, included in

foundation plantings or mixed borders, or massed as a
ground cover. A good transition plant between manicured
gardens and natural areas. Native to moist prairies, it thrives
in dry sites too.

How to Grow
Prefers full sun but tolerates part shade. Thrives with ordinary soil and watering, but tolerates dry, rocky soil. Cut back
or mow in spring so seeds can fall, or propagate by dividing
older plants.

Stipa

sty'puh
Gramineae. Grass family
   Mostly perennial grasses with slender, rough leaves and
usually narrow panicles of flowers, sometimes with very long
hairlike awns that give the inflorescences a silken sheen. The
genus is dubbed needle grass because of sharp-pointed seeds.
About 300 species, widespread around the globe in temperate and warmer regions. Recently reclassified, these grasses
are now mostly assigned to the genus *Nassella*.
   Stipa grasses make excellent specimens in the mixed border or among other grasses. The flowers have a see-through
effect above the large dense clumps of foliage. Translucent
outer coverings remain after the seeds fall, giving a gentle,
flaglike appearance to the grass for many weeks.

■ *cernua*
Nodding feather grass
Zones 8–9. P/Cl/C
Height: 1–2 ft. Spread: 1–2 ft.
   This delicate perennial grass is a western native. No longer
widespread, it can still be seen along the roadsides in the
foothills of the Sierra Nevada and California coastal range.
The breathtaking flowers, which bloom in mid- to late summer, are held high above the foliage. Like similar American
natives feather grass *(Stipa comata)* and purple needlegrass
(S. pulchra), *S. cernua* has long hairlike awns that glisten in
the light like golden threads. Plant in groups for a stunning
effect in a sunlit garden.

How to Grow
Full sun. Well-drained soil; thrives in sandy and rocky sites
as well as in average garden soil and in clay. Drought-tolerant thanks to roots that can reach 15 ft. deep. With additional water, the clumps become more dense. Cut back after

florescences shatter. Stipa species can be tricky to cultivate. They seem to do best where they crop up naturally, in the American West. Grow from seed, or buy young nursery-grown plants. They require several seasons to become dominant; for the first year or two they remain tiny seedlings and need weeding. Once established, a clump may live 200 years.

gigantea p. 176
Giant feather grass
Zones 7–9. P/Cl/C
Height: 2–3 ft. Spread: 3–5 ft.

A cool-season perennial native to Spain, Portugal, and Africa, this fine-textured giant gets its name from its towering panicles of flowers. They stretch up to 4 ft. above the foliage and spread out in a wide sheaf up to 6 ft. across. The show is spectacular, with open, arching panicles of dangling flowers. Each seed is tipped by a long awn that shimmers in sunlight and shivers in the breeze. The grass blooms in late spring to early summer.

How to Grow
Sun. Well-drained, rich soil. Water regularly until the plant is well established. Can be tricky to propagate; it fails to thrive after dividing. Buy young plants and transplant in spring, or plant seed and be patient; it can take months to germinate.

ramosissima 'Pillar of Smoke'
Pillar of smoke
Zones 9–10. P/Cl/C
Height: 6–7 ft. Spread: 3 ft.

One of the newest introductions to American ornamental grasses, this cool-season Australian species grows in a tall, arching clump of fine leaves that emerge from a stand of bamboolike stems. The flowers start blooming in late winter and don't quit until the end of summer. They are finely textured panicles that arch out through the leaves along the entire sheaf of foliage, like wisps of smoke rising from a chimney. This plant has enough stature to work as a specimen, and it is dramatic in groups. A dark background makes the smoky effect outstanding.

How to Grow
Sun. Moist but well-drained soil; adapts to sandy and rocky sites as well as average garden soil. Cut back in fall. The plant's limits of cold tolerance aren't yet known; it may be hardy in Zone 8 or even colder areas. In California, it shows signs of becoming an invasive weed, having escaped from residential plantings to roadsides.

■ **tenuissima** *(see below for photo)*
Mexican feather grass
Zones 7–10. P/Cl/C
Height: 12–18 in. Spread: 12–18 in.

Mexican feather grass has a denser, more fluid look than the open California species. Clumps of extremely fine foliage spray upward and outward. The flowers appear above the foliage in a silky stream, emerging green in late spring to early summer, soon changing to a beautiful yellow-green, then finally to gold. The feathery inflorescences last well into fall and add softness to the garden and indoor arrangements. The cultivar 'Pony Tails' (see photo on p. 176) has abundant and very showy flowers that arch like a horse's silky, flaxen tail. Like other exotic stipas, it may hold the potential for becoming a troublesome weed.

How to Grow
Sun to part shade. Widely adaptable; needs good drainage. Will thrive in lean, sandy, or rocky soils as well as in the garden. Plant seeds or buy young plants and transplant to the garden in spring. Like other stipas, Mexican feather grass resents dividing. It self-sows abundantly, so plant it in a naturalized meadow or other setting where seedlings aren't a problem.

Tridens
try´denz
Gramineae. Grass family

Perennial grasses that grow in tufts or clumps. Flowers vary from tall delicate panicles to fluffy short tufts. Some 15 species, nearly all native to the Americas. Many are common roadside and field grasses.

■ **flavus**
Purple top
Zones 5–10. P/Cl/W
Height: 12–18. Spread: 18–24 in.

This warm-season perennial grows in fairly short clumps of slender foliage that are pleasant enough but nothing special, until deep burgundy flowers arise in late summer. The tall bare-stemmed panicles, so slight that they are barely noticeable close up, are beautiful when seen in a group from a distance, or set off against a light-colored masonry wall. The stems are dark, too, and the inflorescences are shiny. A common wild grass in the lower Midwest, it stretches for miles along unmowed roadsides like a plum-colored pool. The plant is valuable for fall and winter color, too, maturing to a

arm golden tan and holding up the airy panicles through
ne winter. Plant in groups or masses or let it self-sow
nroughout a meadow garden; it's beautiful with native pale
lue asters. Pick the fresh purple flowers for an airy touch in
rrangements.

low to Grow

ull sun to moderate shade. Average garden soil. Also thrives
n heavy clay and lean soils. Tolerates drought. Cut back old
oliage in early spring. Self-sows moderately to generously.
ropagate by seed or divide in early spring.

ripsicum

ip′suh-kum
iramineae. Grass family

Robust perennials with dense, flat leaves. Valuable as for-
ge grasses in the Americas, they were also cultivated for
rain by Central American Indians, who selectively bred *Trip-
icum dactyloides* for an improved harvest. It was once
nought that *Tripsacum* grasses may have been the ancestor
f corn, but today that theory has lost ground because of an
pparent lack of genetic compatibility — even when *Trip-
icum* grows next to corn, the two don't hybridize. At least
ve species, native to the Americas.

dactyloides *p. 177*

iama grass, gamma grass
ones 4–9. P/Cl/W
leight: 6–10 ft. Spread: 6 ft.

The coarse, arching foliage of perennial gama grass grows
n a large, often sprawling clump. The unusual flowers are
lender, fingerlike spikes that arch over the foliage, account-
ng for the Greek name *dactyloides*, which means finger. Male
nd female flowers are separate, a trait unusual to most
rasses but found also in the grass we know as corn *(Zea
iays)*. Both the orange stamens of the male flower, held
bove the females, and the purple stigmas of the female are
ighly noticeable in bloom. This is a big grass that thrives
ear water. Best in groups. Adds interesting texture and
eight to a shade garden.

low to Grow

ull sun to moderate shade. Moist soil, bog gardens, edges of
onds and streams. In the wild usually found in pure stands,
nmixed with other plants; it will also naturalize in the gar-
en. Leaf edges are rough and can cut; use care when work-

ing around them. Cut back after frost kills the foliage. Prop
agate by seed or division in spring. May self-sow.

Typha

ty´fuh
Typhaceae. Cattail family
   These familiar rushlike plants of wet places have wid
grassy leaves and erect, velvety brown pokers of flowers –
the typical cattail. Some 10 species, found around the glob

■ *latifolia*   *p. 177*
Cattail, reedmace
Zones 4–9. P/R
Height: 3–5 ft. Spread: 3 ft. or more
   A perennial that spreads by rhizomatous roots to form
thick colonies at water's edge and in shallow water. It ha
wide, strappy leaves and brown cigar-shaped pokers. Th
spikes persist until seeds fluff out and fly away in fall and win
ter. Foliage turns golden tan then bleaches to beige in winte
   Narrow-leaved cattail *(T. angustifolia)* has a more refine
look than the common cattail *(T. latifolia)*, with slim, fla
leaves and slender brown spikes that are usually about $1/2$ in
wide. The spikes of both species are striking in fresh or drie
arrangements, but spray with clear polyurethane to kee
them from turning to fluff.

How to Grow
Highly invasive. Choose a spot with care; once established
cattails are very difficult, if not impossible, to remove. Grov
in sun, in almost any soil as long as it's wet. Colonizes in we
soil and in shallow water of less than a foot or so deep. Prop
agate by dividing the spreading roots. Let new foliage pus
up through old; it will quickly overtake it. Muskrats are fon
of cattail roots and shoots and may dine on your plantin;
They're fun to watch, and the plants soon recover.

■ *minima*
Dwarf Japanese cattail
Zones 4–9. P/R
Height: 1–2 ft. Spread: 2 ft. or more
   There's no other word for this cattail but cute. About ha
the height of the common pond plant, it spreads more slowl
too. Its short spikes and narrow leaves are perfect for sma
pools and large tubs of mixed water plants. Charming i
arrangements.

How to Grow

Full sun to part or light shade. Adaptable to most soils as long as they are wet. Flourishes in shallow water. Divide in early spring.

Uniola

-nee-oh´luh.

Gramineae. Grass family.

Perennial grasses that spread by creeping rhizomes. Only four species, native to salt flats and sand dunes of North and Central America. Some species formerly classified in this genus have been moved to *Chasmanthium*.

paniculata p. 178

sea oats

Zones 7–10. P/R/W

Height: 3–8 ft. Spread: 3 ft. or more

A beautiful native grass, sea oats once covered the coastal dunes from Virginia to Florida and eastern Texas into Mexico. Today, it's an endangered species in the Southeast because of overpicking, foot traffic, and habitat destruction. Supervised, protected plantings are increasing its tenuous hold in the region. Important as a dune stabilizer, the grass has creeping roots that cover large areas of ground and hold the sand together. Heavy, drooping panicles of seeds start green and ripen to mellow tan. The flat spikelets are very similiar to those of *Chasmanthium latifolium,* wild oats, a grass that makes a good substitute in noncoastal gardens for this graceful, sand-loving native.

How to Grow

Full sun. Must have sand or very sandy soil; only for coastal gardens. Spreads in appropriate conditions by creeping rhizomes. Let it naturalize and avoid fussing with it; the roots are sensitive to disturbance by foot traffic.

Vetiveria

vet-ih-ver´ee-uh

Gramineae. Grass family

Also called vetiver, this genus includes only two species, both of them native to Old World tropical regions.

■ *zizanioides* p. 178
(*Vetiver zizanioides*)
Vetiver
Zones 9–10. P/Cl/W
Height: 4–10 ft. Spread: 4–6 ft.

A large grass that grows in dense tufts of slender leaves. Erect, fluffy panicles of flowers emerge in late summer to early fall. The aromatic, rhizomatous roots yield an oil used in perfumes, and the roots themselves are woven into screens and mats in India. The fragrance of the grass is most pronounced when dampened by the frequent warm rains of these regions. The plant has escaped from cultivation in some areas of the subtropical United States. It can sometimes be found growing wild in Louisiana. The stems are bare near the bottom, so grow this as a background grass with shorter grasses or other tropical plants in front. It's also useful as a hedge or screen, staying evergreen in frost-free climates.

How to Grow
Sun to part shade. Very adaptable. In its native haunts, vetiver grows on riverbanks and in other wet places, but it also thrives in average garden soil and tolerates drought. Cut back frost-killed foliage. Propagate by dividing in early spring.

Yucca
yuk´uh
Agavaceae. Agave family

Woody perennials with short or medium-high trunks and fibrous swordlike leaves. Erect, branched stalks bear large, usually white flowers and woody or fleshy fruits. About 40 species, native to North America. These plants grow in emphatic spiky clumps.

■ *filamentosa* p. 179
Bear grass, Adam's needle
Zones 5–10. P/Cl
Height: 2–3 ft. Spread: 5–6 ft.

This southeastern native is the most commonly offered yucca. It spreads slowly to make a wide patch with many rosettes of sword-shaped foliage. The evergreen leaves have sharp tips and curly fibers along the edges. The tall stalks of white flowers are very showy in June. Gather the woody pods in fall for dried arrangements. Plants sold as *Y. filamentosa* may actually be *Y. flaccida* or *Y. smalliana;* it's hard to distinguish among them.

Yuccas aren't restricted to dry climates or xeriscape gardens. They combine well with perennials or grasses in a sunny bed or border. Individual clumps make a dramatic accent or focal point.

How to Grow

Full sun. Needs well-drained soil; thrives in poor, dry soil as well as average garden soil. Tolerates winter cold, summer heat, and wind. Transplant container-grown plants in spring. Established plants form offsets at the base that can be removed and transplanted. Only care required is the removal of old flower stalks and dead leaves.

Zea

zee´uh
Gramineae. Grass family

These Central American native grasses include only a few species (some authorities say two; others three or four), but their importance to humankind is immense. Maize has been a staple for thousands of years; "new" cultivars are still being developed from ancient grains found at archaeological sites. Male and female flowers are separate; the male flowers are in the tassel that tops the plant, the females in the inflorescences that form at leaf axils and mature into cobs of corn.

■ *mays* *p. 000*
Corn, maize
Zones 4–9. A/W
Height: 3–15 ft. Spread: 2 ft.

This annual grass is a food staple familiar to us as corn but there are dozens of intriguing ornamental varieties that are worth a spot in the garden. The foliage of the plant has a strongly architectural quality and often striking leaf color. Try corn as a hedge or background planting.

Corn is easy to grow in any zone, though some varieties may not ripen their ears in short-season areas. Cultivars with unusual foliage are interesting garden plants in any area. Try 'Albovariegata', with white stripes on its green flags of leaves; 'Variegata', with stripes of creamy yellow or pinkish; 'Quadricolor', with fantastic foliage coloring of white, yellow, green and pink. 'Red Stalker' has striking red and purple stalks. 'Harlequin' has beautiful deep red ears and leaves with red stripes. The many varieties of "Indian corn" also often show good red or purple coloring in their foliage; look for specialty heritage seed sources to find more unusual varieties with kernels in gleaming pink, steel blue, turquoise, deep red, and other hues.

How to Grow

Full sun. Rich, moist but well-drained soil. Plant seeds directly where they are to grow. Many gardeners look for young oak leaves as a sign that the time is right for planting. If you're planning to use the ears for decorative purposes, let them dry on the plant. Cultivars hybridize freely, since pollen is wind-carried. It's fun to try saving seed, or to try planting seed from an ear of ornamental corn that you've found elsewhere, but if you grow more than one kind of corn in your garden (or if there are neighboring farm fields), be aware that the seeds may not come true.

Appendices

Hardiness Zone Map

Zone 1	below -50°		**Zone 6**	-10° to 0°
Zone 2	-50° to -40°		**Zone 7**	0° to 10°
Zone 3	-40° to -30°		**Zone 8**	10° to 20°
Zone 4	-30° to -20°		**Zone 9**	20° to 30°
Zone 5	-20° to -10°		**Zone 10**	30° to 40°
			Zone 11	above 40°

Sources of Seeds and Plants

Every year local nurseries offer a greater variety of ornamental grasses, but many of the grasses in this book will be available to you only through specialty mail-order suppliers like those listed below. You can order from them directly or through your local nursery. If you live nearby or are traveling in the area, be aware that some have demonstration gardens open to the public; phone to find out.

Kurt Bluemel, Inc.
2740 Greene Lane
Baldwin, MD 21013-9523
(410) 557-7229

Bluestem Prairie Nursery
13197 E. 13th Rd.
Hillsboro, IL 62049
(217) 532-6344

Carroll Gardens, Inc.
444 East Main St.
P.O. Box 310
Westminster, MD 21157
(800) 638-6334

Crownsville Nursery
P.O. Box 797
Crownsville, MD 21032
(410) 849-3143

The Flowery Branch Seed Company
P.O. Box 1330
Flowery Branch, GA 30542
(770) 536-8380

Greenlee Nursery
257 E. Franklin Ave.
Pomona, CA 91766
Fax only (909) 620-9283

Seeds Trust High Altitude Gardens
P.O. Box 1048
4150 Black Oak Dr.
Hailey, ID 83333
(208) 788-4363

Klehm Nursery
4210 N. Duncan Rd.
Champaign, IL 61821
(800) 553-3715

Limerock Ornamental Grasses, Inc.
70 Sawmill Rd.
Port Matilda, PA 16870
(814) 692-2272

Maryland Aquatic Nurseries
3427 N. Furnace Rd.
Jarrettsville, MD 21084
(410) 557-7615

Midwest Groundcovers
P.O. Box 748
St. Charles, IL 60174
(847) 742-1790

Milaeger's Gardens
4838 Douglas Ave.
Racine, WI 53402-2498
(800) 669-6956

Mostly Natives Nursery
P.O. Box 258
27235 Hwy. 1
Tomales, CA 94971
(707) 878-2009

Plants of the Southwest
Aqua Fria, Rt. 6, Box 11A
Santa Fe, NM 87501
(800) 788-7333

Prairie Moon Nursery
Rt. 3, Box 163
Winona, MN 55987
(Native grasses only)
(507) 452-1362

Prairie Nursery
P.O. Box 306
Westfield, WI 53964
(Native grasses)
(608) 296-3679

Shady Oaks Nursery
112 10th Ave. S.E.
Waseca, MN 56093
(507) 835-5033

Trans Pacific Nursery
16065 Oldsville Rd.
McMinnville, OR 97128
(503) 472-6215

White Flower Farm
P.O. Box 50
Litchfield, CT 06759-0050
(800) 503-9624

WHOLESALE ONLY
(Order through a local
nursery.)

**Native Sons Wholesale
Nursery, Inc.**
379 West El Campo Rd.
Arroyo Grande, CA 93420
(805) 481-5996

Sunny Border Nurseries, Inc.
1709 Kensington Rd.
P.O. Box 483
Kensington, CT 06037
(800) 732-1627

Photo Credits

Cathy Wilkinson Barash/Photo/Nats: 129A

C. Colston Burrell: 98–99, 126A, 128B, 130A

Priscilla Connell/Photo/Nats: 178A

Michael Dirr: 117B, 133B, 172A

Thomas Eltzroth: 72–73, 129B, 131A, 153A, 170B

Derek Fell: 46–47, 48–49, 52–53, 56–57, 68–69, 70–71, 74–75, 76–77, 78–79, 88–89, 90–91, 92–93, 94–95, 100–101, 106, 118A, B, 121A, 124B, 125B, 126B, 127A, B, 134A, B, 136A, B, 137B, 138B, 140A, 141B, 144A, B, 145A, 146A, B, 147B, 148A, B, 149B, 150A, B, 151A, 156B, 159A, B, 160B, 161A, 162B, 163A, B, 164A, B, 166A, 167B, 168B, 169B, 173B, 174A, 175B, 176B, 177A, B, 178B, 179B

Dency Kane: 58–59, 116A, 125A, 165A, 170A

Charles Mann: 50–51, 104–105, 110–111, 119A, B, 122B, 123A, B, 124A, 131B, 160A, 161B, 171B

Jerry Pavia: 54, 55, 60–61, 80, 81, 84–85, 86–87, 96–97, 102–103, 107, 108–109, 112–113, 120A, 122A, 139A, 142A, 145B, 156A, 158A, 165B, 167A, 169A

Ben Phillips/Photo/Nats: 133A, 147A, 152A, 178A

PhotoSynthesis: 82–83, 117A, 120B, 121B, 128A, 132A, B, 137A, 162A

Steven Still: 62–63, 64–65, 66–67, 130B, 135A, B, 138A, 139B, 140B, 141A, 142B, 143A, B, 149A, 151B, 152B, 153B, 154A, B, 155A, B, 157A, B, 158B, 166B, 168A, 171A, 172B, 173A, 174B, 175A, 176A, 179A

Index

Titles available in the Taylor's Guide series:

At your bookstore or by calling 1-800-225-3362